P9-EMQ-582

DATE DUE			

921
LEE

31286111051968
Robertson, James I.

Robert E. Lee :
Virginia soldier,
American citizen

Robert E. Lee

VIRGINIAN SOLDIER ★ AMERICAN CITIZEN

Robert E. Lee

JAMES I. ROBERTSON JR.

Atheneum Books for Young Readers New York London Toronto Sydney

Atheneum Books for Young Readers
An imprint of Simon & Schuster Children's Publishing Division
1230 Avenue of the Americas
New York, New York 10020

Book design by Liana M. Zamora
The text for this book is set in Caslon 540.

Manufactured in the United States of America
2 3 4 5 6 7 8 9 10

Library of Congress Cataloging-in-Publication Data
Robertson, James I.
Robert E. Lee : Virginian soldier, American citizen /
James I. Robertson Jr.—1st ed.
v. cm.
CONTENTS: The making of a soldier—Nation vs. country—Rocky path to army
commander—Brilliance in the field—The bloodiest day—Loss of an arm—
Gettysburg—Forced on the defensive—From siege to defeat—National symbol.
ISBN-13: 978-0-689-85731-7
ISBN-10: 0-689-85731-4
1. Lee, Robert E. (Robert Edward), 1807-1870—Juvenile literature. 2. Generals—
Confederate States of America—Biography—Juvenile literature. 3. Confederate
States of America. Army—Biography—Juvenile literature. 4. United States—
History—Civil War, 1861-1865—Campaigns—Juvenile literature.
[1. Lee, Robert E. (Robert Edward), 1807-1870. 2. Generals. 3. Confederate
States of America. 4. United States—History—Civil War, 1861-1865.] I. Title.
E467.1.L4R625 2005
973.7'3'092—dc22   2003022108

To great Americans
of the past from whom
we can learn so much
for the future

Contents

Acknowledgments

THE BEST PART OF WRITING A BOOK IS SAYING THANKS TO THOSE WHO HAVE EAGERLY HELPED ALONG the way. I have benefited from such friends.

Research and writing costs were defrayed by funds established at Virginia Polytechnic Institute and State University by two now-deceased but never-forgotten friends, J. Ambler Johnston and Frank L. Curtis.

To critique the manuscript, I asked Virginia Tech students in my advanced Civil War course to recommend any outstanding teachers under whom they had studied in high school. The following educators, best among the best, each contributed much to the improvement of this book: Andy Buckman, Indian Valley, Virginia; Martha Buckman, Staunton, Virginia; Pam McConnell, Hixson, Tennessee; Susan Orr, Springfield, Virginia; and Marty Potts, Purcellville, Virginia. Suzanne W. Silek, former president of the Virginia Division of the United Daughters of the Confederacy, likewise gave the manuscript a careful reading with the eye of the good historian she is.

Gary M. Worley and John A. Baird of Virginia Tech's Digital Imaging Department displayed anew their craftsmanship in the preparation of the majority of illustrations contained herein.

Doing a second study for Atheneum Books for Young Readers was a pleasure, thanks to Ginee Seo and editorial assistant Kristy Raffensberger. Their cooperation and enthusiasm eased the long path of work between premise and publication.

As always, my best friend and the mother of my children was there to assist in any way. No greater helpmate could exist than Libba.

Robert E. Lee will appear on any short list of great Americans. His name and fame continue to sweep across the ages. Hopefully, for young Americans studying the past to find their beacons for the future, this introduction to Lee will be both enriching and inspiring.

–James I. Robertson Jr.
November 2005

Photograph of General Lee and his signature.

Introduction

MAY 3, 1863, WAS THE SECOND BLOODIEST DAY OF THE ENTIRE CIVIL WAR. BATTLE RAGED IN woods and fields as two mighty armies fought and killed at Chancellorsville, Virginia. The Union line broke. Confederates surged forward to the key point on the battlefield: the now-burning Chancellor tavern that had been Union army headquarters.

In the midst of the gun smoke, flames, and destruction, General Robert E. Lee rode to the front of the lines. An aide to the general described that moment: "One long, unbroken cheer, in which the feeble cry of those who lay helpless on the earth blended with the strong voices of those who still fought, rose high above the roar of battle, and hailed the presence of the victorious chief. He sat in the full realization of all that soldiers dream of—triumph; and as I looked upon him in the complete fruition of the success which his genius, courage, and confidence in his army had won, I thought that it must have been from such a scene that men in ancient days rose to the dignity of gods."[1]

War always brings an awareness of heroes who make history. We must look back for guidance and strength because we cannot see the unknowns that lie ahead. In turning to the past, one does not have to search far before the imposing figure of Robert E. Lee comes into view. He stands too large to be overlooked. Next to George Washington and Abraham Lincoln, Lee is America's most respected historical figure. Standard high school and college textbooks treat him almost with reverence.

Many Americans have difficulty in understanding why this is so. After all, Washington established the nation; Lincoln preserved it; but Lee became the most dangerous opponent the United States ever faced. One of the country's most respected historians concluded: "Robert E. Lee is America's great tragic hero.... He was a marvelously gifted soldier and an ardently devoted patriot, yet he defended the most unacceptable of American causes, secession and slavery, and he suffered the most un-American of experiences, defeat."[2]

This military commander led a revolution against a nation. It failed. That Lee is held in such high esteem by American citizens today is remarkable. It is also a lasting tribute to the Virginian.

Lee's supreme being impressed everyone who ever knew him. Viscount Wolseley, commander in chief of the British armies, met Lee on several occasions during the Civil War. Years later the English soldier declared: "I never felt my own individual insignificance more keenly than I did in his presence." Wolseley added: "I have met many of the great men of my time, but Lee alone impressed me with the feeling that I was in the presence of a man who was cast in a grander mould, and made of different and of finer metal than all other men."[3]

A Lee legend exists today. The legend would not be there if those who knew him had not expressed universal admiration. His bravery, his modesty, his dignity and piety, each added luster to his image. Lee was the first American general ever to lose a war. But defeat itself only enhanced the Lee legend. His exalted character seemed to give respectability to the Confederate cause. The faith he possessed became an abiding expression of God's will on the vanquished. The result has been an elevation of Robert E. Lee to near sainthood. Lee would be horrified at such adoration.

Nevertheless, when New York University established a national Hall of Fame for Great Americans in 1901, Lee was among the first to be inducted. A year later Charles Francis Adams, a former Union officer and descendant of two American presidents, told a Boston audience that it was time for a national monument to Lee. If Lee was a traitor, Adams declared, so too was Washington.[4]

The words Lee so often used—duty, honor, valor—have a quaint sound in much of America today because they are unfamiliar. Some people even assert that no one like Lee could possibly have existed. They say this because no one like him exists today.

He was one of the nation's greatest soldiers. For three decades he served America well. Then, when his homeland—Virginia—left the Union, Lee gave four years of his life and much of his health in fighting that Union. The Confederate States of America lasted as long as it did because of Lee. When he surrendered in 1865, the Southern experience of independence ceased to exist.

Lee not only accepted defeat gracefully; he dedicated the remaining five years of his life to training students—and their parents—to be useful Americans. At his death in 1870 an entire nation mourned. Thousands of people annually come to his grave to pay simple homage.

History is so often a paradox, and Lee in many ways is one of the most puzzling of all the men whom the world terms "superior." In the most tumultuous years of the young Republic, only rarely did emotion disturb his calmness. He was a brilliant army commander; he was also a gentle soul who would not tolerate anyone abusing an animal. He looked to the God of Mankind as he labored beneath the God of Battle. He sought victory over a Union he loved. He won some of the most smashing successes in American military history, but so void of malice was his heart that he customarily referred to the enemy as "our friends across the river."

To any generation, Lee would be a sterling gift. We remember him because he is unforgettable.

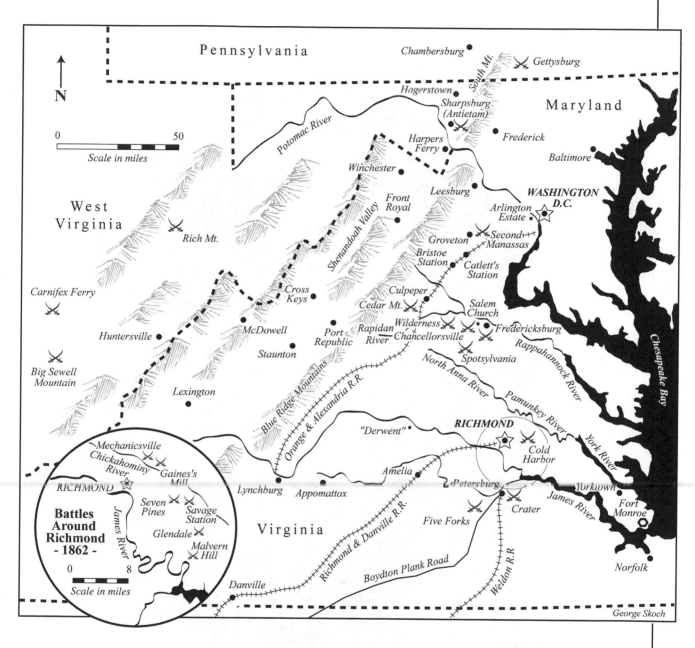

Pennsylvania

West Virginia

Maryland

N

0   50
Scale in miles

Chambersburg

South Mt. ⚔ Gettysburg

Hagerstown

Sharpsburg (Antietam) ⚔

Frederick

Harpers Ferry ⚔

Baltimore

Potomac River

Winchester

Front Royal

Leesburg

Shenandoah Valley

Rich Mt. ⚔

Arlington Estate ⚔ **WASHINGTON D.C.**

Carnifex Ferry ⚔

Cross Keys ⚔

Groveton ⚔ Second Manassas

Bristoe Station

Catlett's Station

Culpeper

Cedar Mt. ⚔

Salem Church

Huntersville

McDowell

Port Republic

Rapidan River

Wilderness ⚔

Chancellorsville ⚔

Fredericksburg

Rappahannock River

Big Sewell Mountain ⚔

Staunton

Blue Ridge Mountains

Spotsylvania ⚔

Chesapeake Bay

Lexington

North Anna River

Pamunkey River

Orange & Alexandria R.R.

"Derwent" ▪

RICHMOND ☆

Cold Harbor ⚔

York River

Mechanicsville ⚔
Chickahominy River
Gaines's Mill ⚔

RICHMOND ☆

Seven Pines ⚔

Savage Station ⚔

Glendale ⚔

James River

Malvern Hill ⚔

Battles Around Richmond - 1862 -

0   8
Scale in miles

Lynchburg

Appomattox

Amelia

Petersburg

Yorktown

Crater ⚔

James River

Fort Monroe

Virginia

Richmond & Danville R.R.

Five Forks ⚔

Weldon R.R.

Danville

Boydton Plank Road

Norfolk

George Skoch

Above: **As a field commander, Lee spent his Civil War career in what was called the Eastern Theater of Operations. Battle sites are shown with crossed swords.**

Above: Robert E. Lee's father, Henry Lee (1756-1818) became governor of the most powerful state in the new American republic. His wife, Ann Hill Carter, was the daughter of the richest plantation owner in Virginia.

The Making of a Soldier

THE LEE FAMILY AND THE VIRGINIA COLONY MARRIED EARLY. IN 1641, ONLY THIRTY-FOUR YEARS after the first English settlers came permanently to the New World, Richard Lee planted his roots in tidewater Virginia soil. He had received an appointment as colonial secretary to the royal governor. In that capacity Richard Lee developed a large and beautiful estate in Westmoreland County alongside the Potomac River. Soon the "Lees of Virginia," as the family was called, fanned out in every direction. They came to represent all that was colonial Virginia aristocracy. New England's John Adams, second president of the United States, asserted that the Lee family had "more men of merit in it than any other family in America."[1]

Henry Lee, the great-grandson of Richard Lee, continued that tradition. When the American Revolution began, he declared: "Virginia is my country. Her will I obey, however lamentable the fate to which it may subject me."[2] He did defend his country, gallantly. Henry Lee was the famous "Light Horse Harry" Lee who commanded George Washington's cavalry.

Wartime fame led to Lee being elected to three terms as governor of Virginia. In 1793 the thirty-seven-year-old Lee married twenty-year-old Ann Hill Carter. Her father was the wealthiest man in Virginia. Carters and Lees had held dominant positions in politics and society for one hundred and fifty years. Two lines of aristocracy came together.

George Washington died in 1799 while Lee was serving in the U.S. Congress. Lee would always be remembered as the man who eulogized Washington as "first in war, first in peace, and first in the hearts of his countrymen."[3]

Stratford, the name of the ancestral Lee estate in Westmoreland County, became a symbol of Virginia society. Henry Lee was master there: charming in company, brilliant in politics, and devoted to his family. For all of his good graces, however, Henry Lee could not resist the temptation to speculate in land and business. Debt was no stranger to tidewater gentry, but Henry Lee lost most of his friends through reckless dealings. He even attempted to pass off a valueless note to his hero, Washington.[4]

Bad business ventures soon left Lee and his family destitute. It was in such an atmosphere, on January 19, 1807, that Ann Carter Lee gave birth to the last of five children. His life began in the same bedroom in which two uncles—Richard Henry Lee and Francis Lightfoot Lee—had been born. Both were signers of the Declaration of Independence. The baby was named Robert Edward after two of Mrs. Lee's brothers. Robert Lee was two years old when his father went to jail because of bad debts. (Under the curious laws of that day, a man who owed large sums went to prison without a chance to pay off his obligations.)

Relatives came to Henry Lee's aid, and he gained his release after a year in jail. Yet he had to abandon Stratford. At the departure from the ancestral estate, four-year-old Robert Lee's last farewell was to two angels etched in an iron fireback in the small fireplace in the nursery.[5] The family moved into a small home in the nearby town of Alexandria.

In 1812, Robert's father opposed the popular war with England. He openly supported a young Baltimore editor who was writing antiwar editorials. One summer night a drunken mob sought to destroy the printing shop. Henry Lee was there; and in the fighting that followed, a hoodlum dripped hot candle wax into Lee's eyes and tried to cut off his nose. Left for dead, Lee was rescued by friends the next morning.

The badly injured Lee never fully recovered from the assault. His face was disfigured, his health broken, his fortunes almost nonexistent.

In 1813, Lee sailed for Barbados in the West Indies. He hoped to regain his strength and his wealth. Only failure greeted his efforts. Lee was struggling home in 1818 when he died on Cumberland Island, Georgia.

Robert Lee had little recollection of his father. What he never forgot was the faded financial condition of his family. His mother more than compensated for the absence of the father. Mrs. Lee taught her son the values of respect, faith, self-control, responsibility, and careful management. She sacrificed and saved to maintain an appearance of social grace. Robert Lee grew up in a genteel poverty. While respectful of his father's memory, the son looked always to George Washington for inspiration. The Lee family worshipped in the Alexandria church that Washington had attended. Scores of townspeople filled the lad with stories of what a great man Washington was, especially during his final years at the Mount Vernon estate not far from town.

Washington literally became Robert Lee's role model. In later years, army commander Lee would wear a colonel's uniform because army commander Washington had done so. When Lee acquired a new horse in 1861, he would name it Traveller after a mount Washington had ridden. Much of Lee's military thinking came from the man known as "the father of his country."

Lee's childhood was fairly pleasant. Frequent visits from Alexandria to the Carter family's Shirley Plantation on the James River gave Robert Lee a somewhat cosmopolitan view of life. He became the chief servant for a mother whose health began to decline early. Young Robert shopped and cooked; he carried his mother to a carriage and set the cushions to her liking before taking her for a ride.

Formal education began with a plantation school, a private tutor, and the highly regarded Alexandria Academy. This was as good a preparatory education as existed in early nineteenth-century Virginia. Choosing his course of life was a process of elimination. As the youngest of three sons, no inheritance was waiting for him. A business career was not tempting because upper society looked down on the world of trade. Young Lee's Episcopal faith was barely formed, so the ministry was

Below: **Stratford Hall was the ancestral home where Lee was born. Located on white cliffs overlooking the Potomac River, the estate at one time consisted of 4,800 acres.**

unappealing. Merely obtaining a college degree offered little promise for the future. Lee, remembering both Washington and his father, decided to go into the military.

The best place to start was the U.S. Military Academy. Lee had no difficulty in securing an appointment. His family name, educational background, and quick, precise mind made him fully qualified. President James Monroe issued the appointment. In the spring of 1825, Secretary of War John C. Calhoun directed Lee to report to West Point.

The school is forty miles north of New York City, in a majestic setting on bluffs overlooking the Hudson River. Established in 1802, the academy consisted then of four gray stone buildings on an open plain. Two of the structures were barracks, one was a mess hall, and one a two-story, multipurpose building housing classrooms, the library, a laboratory, and the chapel.

Some 200 cadets there studied engineering slanted toward tactics and military architecture, along with the "science" of artillery. They learned military organization, customs of marching, battlefield formations, and the basic principles of war. Military architecture centered on the construction of forts, bridges, and canals.

West Point was the finest military academy and engineering school in the Western Hemisphere. It was also a school that instilled discipline and molded character.

Lee became as close to a model cadet as the academy has ever had. Neatness, diligence, good conduct, and patience were absolutely necessary for a successful cadet. Lee possessed them all. He was among the top five students in his class throughout his four years of study.

In his senior year he held the rank of cadet adjutant—the highest status a West Point student could earn. Not one demerit ever went on his record. This shows how orderly and organized his nature was. He studiously obeyed all rules and regulations. More important, as a young man he displayed a confidence that gave him perfect discipline in a school atmosphere where behavior was one of the most important ingredients for graduation.

Right: **Mary Anne Randolph Custis (1808-1873) was only slightly younger than her husband, Robert. She was a spirited woman with bright eyes, a sense of humor, and strong powers of conversation.**

If any jealousy of Lee existed among fellow cadets, it has never come to light. Indeed, the Virginian seems to have been a favorite with everyone. Joseph E. Johnston, one of Lee's classmates, stated years later: "No other youth or man united the qualities that win warm friendship and command high respect. For he was full of sympathy and kindness, genial and fond of gay conversations . . . while his correctness of demeanor and language and attention to all duties . . . gave him a superiority that every one acknowledged in his heart."[6]

Erasmus D. Keyes, three years behind Lee at West Point, observed after a career as a Union general that all of Lee's "accomplishments and alluring virtues appeared natural to him, and he was free from the anxiety, distrust and awkwardness that attend a sense of inferiority."[7] Keyes instantly recognized what others would come to see: Nothing about Lee was artificial or manufactured.

Lee graduated second in the West Point class of 1829.[8] He looked like a soldier. At a time when the average male was 5 feet, 7 inches tall and weighed 135 pounds, Lee stood 5 feet, 11 inches tall and carried 170 pounds on a muscular frame. He was broad-shouldered and erect, with the brown eyes and black hair of the Lee family. His manner was outgoing. The quiet, composed nature that history remembers would come years later.

High standing in his class brought Lee an appointment to the Engineer Corps. It was the elite branch of the U.S. Army. Members received extra pay. Because the federal government assisted in public projects, engineering officers had the luxury of assignments close to urban areas rather than being posted to lonely vigils on the frontier.

During the War of 1812, Americans had made a brilliant defense at Fort McHenry. (Francis Scott Key wrote a poem about the action in Baltimore harbor, and his words became the lyrics of "The Star-Spangled Banner.") That heroic stand convinced military officials that similar forts should be built at strategic spots all along the Atlantic coast.

Lee's first orders were to proceed to Cockspur Island, near Savannah, Georgia. There he was to assist in the first construction of what became Fort Pulaski at the mouth of the Savannah River. Lee cared for his ailing mother in her last days, then started south. He was among the first generation of Lees in Virginia who would be dependent upon what money they could earn away from plantation life.

A second tour of duty began in 1831 at Fortress Monroe, on the northern side of the great Virginia harbor of Hampton Roads. This new duty brought Lee to only a day's trip by steamboat from his family in Alexandria. The more he visited home, the deeper the twenty-four-year-old lieutenant fell in love with a childhood friend. Mary Anne Randolph Custis was the spoiled daughter of Mr. and Mrs. George Washington Parke Custis. The father was the grandson of Mrs. George Washington and the adopted son of Washington himself. Mary was

Below: **Fortress Monroe, Virginia, was a premier army installation in the early nineteenth century. Its location was at the mouth of both Chesapeake Bay and Norfolk Harbor.**

slender, attractive, and a year younger than Robert. Her family owned four tracts of land. One was the imposing Arlington estate that overlooked the Potomac River. The home contained many belongings of General Washington. Directly across the river was Washington, D.C., the national capital.

Mary Custis had known a life of luxury at Arlington. As the only surviving Custis child, she someday would inherit the Custis fortune. Yet it was not wealth that attracted Lee. He saw sparkling eyes, a winning smile, a Virginia lady with charm and grace. Mary in turn was captivated by the young, handsome, obviously capable army officer who never gambled or used tobacco and, except for an occasional glass of wine, did not drink.

On June 30, 1831, a new bonding of a Washington and a Lee occurred. The wedding took place at Arlington. It was probably the most festive occasion ever held at the great mansion.

A monthlong honeymoon followed. Lee refused to depend on the wealth of Mary's family. The two would live on his army pay. The young couple then settled into two rooms of a Fortress Monroe barracks. Lieutenant Lee became one of the most popular men at the post. A cousin wrote that "my eye fell upon his face in perfect repose and the thought at once flashed through my mind: 'you certainly look more like a great man than anyone I have ever seen.'"[9]

Lee was quite content at Fortress Monroe in his beloved homeland. Mary Custis Lee was not. Accustomed to wealthy surroundings,

servants, and a gay, carefree life, she found living on a somber army post to be unusually dull and boring. Cleaning house and fixing meals were new and unhappy chores for her. She longed for Arlington.

In September 1832 the first Lee child was born. The boy was christened George Washington Custis. Mrs. Lee then went to Arlington for Christmas holidays that extended well into the following year. The couple would have six other children: Mary (born in 1835), William Henry Fitzhugh (1837), Ann (1839), Agnes (1841), Robert Edward Jr. (1843), and Mildred (1845).

Lee had a genuine love of children, and youngsters in turn were attracted to him. The seven offspring and many other financial obligations caused Lee to worry about being able to live off his army salary. He was always careful with expenditures and was not given to waste or extravagance. His only personal indulgence was in handsome uniforms.

Throughout those years Mrs. Lee remained for the most part at Arlington. The separations from her husband were many and long. Yet the couple never ceased in their genuine love for each other.

Meanwhile, Lee moved from one unexciting duty to another. In 1834 he left Fortress Monroe to become an assistant to the head

The Making of a Soldier

of the Engineer Corps. Three years later he went to St. Louis to help in improving the river channels of that great Mississippi River port. Lee was the man most responsible for keeping the river flowing smoothly by St. Louis.

The assignment took three years to complete. Mayor John F. Darby was much impressed with the way Lee worked. Darby noted that Lee "went in person with the hands every morning about sunrise, and worked day by day in the hot, broiling sun. . . . He shared in the hard task and common fare and rations furnished to the common laborers. . . . He maintained and preserved under all circumstances his dignity and gentlemanly bearing, winning and commanding the esteem, regard, and respect of every one under him."[10]

Promotion to captain came in 1838. "I do not know whether I ought to rejoice or not," Lee wrote home. He longed to return to Virginia. However, he added, "I suppose the more comfortably I am fixed in the army, the less likely I shall be to leave it."[11]

In 1841, Lee began a five-year tour of duty repairing the defenses of Fort Hamilton at the mouth of the harbor at New York City. All of these engineering assignments from Savannah to St. Louis to New York taught Lee several things. He became good at a variety of challenges. At the same time, he learned how to get along with people of every type. As his patience grew, so did a sense of humor.

Lee also accepted dutifully the long periods of loneliness without his ever-increasing family.

Each new child was welcomed but an added responsibility. One authority stated: "Every sickness of any of his children was an anxiety, each injury to them an agony to him."[12] The sons all proved high-spirited and slow to acquire the self-discipline that was the very foundation of their father's life.

Early in 1846, Lee received a short-term appointment to the Board of Examiners of the graduating cadets at West Point. This duty brought him into company with the man who would have a great effect on his life: Winfield Scott, General-in-Chief of the U.S. Army. At a glance, the two men seemed to have little in common. Lee was young, handsome, modest, quiet by nature. Scott was twenty years older, a huge man with elaborate uniforms, strong opinions never concealed, and a flashing temper when aroused. The two officers saw each other daily. Lee displayed the same respect and attention to duty he always had. Scott watched him closely and developed a genuine, almost fatherlike affection for his fellow Virginian.

Life for everyone in the army changed in May 1846, when a long quarrel between the United States and Mexico turned into violence.

A decade earlier the province of Texas had successfully revolted against Mexico. In 1845

Opposite: **Antonio Lopez de Santa Anna (1794-1876) commanded the Mexican Army in the war against the United States. The general was a blend of charisma and arrogance. While he could always raise troops for his army, he was constantly in need of money.**

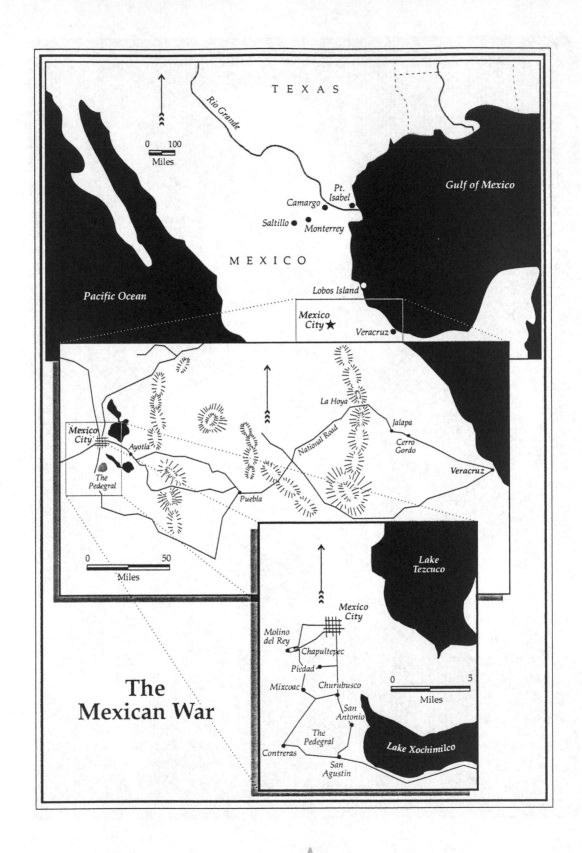

TEXAS

Rio Grande

Gulf of Mexico

0   100
Miles

Pt.
Isabel
Camargo
Saltillo   Monterrey

MEXICO

Pacific Ocean

Lobos Island

Mexico
City ★
Veracruz

La Hoya
Jalapa
Cerro
Gordo
National Road
Mexico
City
Ayotla
The Pedegral
Puebla
Veracruz

0   50
Miles

Lake
Tezcuco

Mexico
City
Molino
del Rey
Chapultepec
Piedad
Mixcoac   Churubusco
San
Antonio
The
Pedegral
Contreras
San
Agustin

0   5
Miles

Lake Xochimilco

The
Mexican War

the U.S. Congress had admitted Texas to the Union. Yet Mexico still claimed the area. Continuing arguments led to shouting, and shouting eventually led to shooting. Congress declared war on America's southern neighbor.

Seventeen years in the army had prepared Lee for the war that could be a major test of his full abilities as a soldier. In August 1846, he received orders to proceed to San Antonio, Texas. He was to be an assistant engineer with the American forces commanded by General John E. Wool in northern Mexico. Prior to his departure Lee wrote his will. All of his property was to go to Mrs. Lee. At her death the estate would be distributed equally among the children. Lee never changed that simple document.[13]

For two uneventful months after reaching Mexico, Lee taught inexperienced soldiers how to build bridges and to repair roads. It soon became clear that the decisive campaign of the war would be hundreds of miles to the south and led by General Winfield Scott. Lee began to feel that he was going to miss the major action. Pessimism turned to pleasure when, in mid-January 1847, he received orders to proceed to the coastal area around Veracruz and report to chief engineer Colonel Joseph G. Totten.

There Lee strengthened friendships with some of the most promising officers in the army: his West Point friend Joseph E. Johnston; a dark Louisianian with eagle eyes, P. G. T. Beauregard; capable but grumpy George G. Meade; and a

brilliant redheaded lieutenant fresh out of West Point, George B. McClellan. More happily, Lee was assigned to Scott's staff. General and captain quickly renewed their friendship begun two years previously at West Point. Before many weeks Lee was in a small circle of staff officers Scott called his "little cabinet."[14]

Scott's battle plan in Mexico was simple but dangerous. American ships were blockading Veracruz, the country's major seaport. Scott would land troops and capture the city. If this movement did not cause the Mexican government to ask for peace, Scott would lead his army on a 200-mile march through enemy country to the capital of Mexico City. Its seizure would unquestionably end the war.

On March 9 the campaign began when Scott made the first amphibious landing in American military history. Troops stormed ashore several miles south of Veracruz. Staff officers do not normally see much action in battle. Yet Scott relied heavily on his young aides for advice as well as for activities.

A week after Americans established their beachhead on the Mexican coast, Scott sent Captain Lee and Lieutenant Beauregard to scout the approaches to Veracruz and to determine the placement of artillery. The two

Opposite: **These three maps of the Mexican War show the Texas-Mexico region** *(top),* **the advance route to Mexico City** *(center),* **and the battles waged for the Mexican capital** *(bottom).*

officers were returning from the front on a narrow path through thick brush. Suddenly, as they rounded a bend, a sentinel stepped forward just yards away and called: "Halt! Who goes there?"

"Friends!" Lee shouted.

Highly excited, the sentinel fired point-blank at Lee. The musket ball passed between Lee's arm and chest, ripping his uniform coat. Had the wild shot been a fraction of an inch more to the left, Lee would have been killed. The captain sought to overlook the incident, but Scott ordered the young soldier punished for the near tragedy.[15]

During March–September 1847, Scott conducted a dazzling campaign as he moved steadily toward the Mexican capital. Lee displayed heroic conduct throughout the operations. His first act of gallantry came a month into the march.

The Mexican commander, General Antonio López de Santa Anna, made his first concentrated stand at a narrow, rocky pass known as Cerro Gordo. Some 12,000 entrenched Mexicans awaited 10,000 struggling American soldiers. Scott ordered Lee to take a guide and try to work his way around the Mexican left flank. Lee crawled through thick underbrush to get a better look at the position of the Mexican forces. Without warning, he came to a spring being used by enemy soldiers to refill their canteens.

Lee froze for a moment, then crept behind a fallen log. He lay there all day as Mexicans used the log for a bench. Heat and mosquitoes added pain to anxiety. When darkness fell, Lee made his way back to Scott with valuable information.[16]

His recommendation was that Scott's army turn Santa Anna's position by circling around the opponent's left flank. This would cut communication lines and force the Mexicans from their earthworks. Scott fought the battle according to Lee's suggestion. On April 17, Americans attacked Santa Anna's army. Lee guided troops in the attempt to outflank the Mexican line. The terrain was extremely difficult. Lee was leading the troops around great boulders and through ravines when they came under enemy fire.

Lee promptly took charge of directing artillery in this, his first battle. The American cannons raked the Mexican lines. Fighting lasted three hours. Soon the Mexican path of retreat became threatened by Lee's turning movement. Santa Anna retreated from his position. The Americans had gained a major victory. The flanking movement spearheaded by Lee had been the key to success.

In August, Scott's army reached San Augustin. Mexico City was barely ten miles away. Scott paused to determine the best approach to the capital. Directly ahead of his front line was "the *pedregal*," a ten-square-mile, lava-strewn wilderness. One American soldier likened it to "a sea, which having been lashed into fury by a tempest, had been suddenly transformed . . . into stone."[17] The two

Above: Lee's bravery both as a scout
and as an artillery commander enabled
the Americans to win a major victory
at Cerro Gordo.

roads leading through the *pedregal* were heavily defended.

At Scott's directive, on August 19, Lee led some 500 men along an unused wagon trail. The group was able to cross the lava field, hack its way through thick brush, and establish a vantage point for bombarding the Mexican positions. Lee supervised the placement of artillery. He next spent the night crossing and recrossing the *pedregal* in pouring rain. Seven other engineering officers failed to make it. Lightning flashes and Lee's sense of direction were all that kept him from getting lost. Scott would later call those solo trips "the greatest feat of physical and moral courage" in the entire Mexican War.[18]

The climactic battle of the war came on September 13 at Chapultepec, the great stone fortress defending Mexico City. Again Lee seemed everywhere on the field, despite the fact that he had gone forty-eight hours without sleep. At some point he received a flesh wound. It was not life-threatening, but it did involve considerable loss of blood. As Americans were on the verge of victory Scott sent Lee with a message to General William Worth on the front line. Lee successfully made his way through the line of battle. He

Right: The American triumph at the battle of Chapultepec brought the fall of Mexico City and the end of the war. Lee was conspicuous throughout this fight.

returned to Scott, saluted, then toppled from his horse in a faint because of loss of blood and complete exhaustion.[19]

Mexico City fell into American hands, and the war ended. The Duke of Wellington declared Scott to be "the greatest living soldier" for conducting a campaign "unsurpassed in military annals."[20] Lieutenant Richard Ewell thought otherwise. After the fighting ceased, Ewell wrote his brother: "I really think one of the most talented men connected with this army is Captain Lee, of the Engineers. By his daring reconnaissance pushed up to the cannon's mouth, he has enabled General Scott to fight his battles almost without leaving his tent."[21]

Scott was even more lavish with his praise. In his official report of the Mexican operations the general in chief called Lee "the very best soldier I ever saw in the field."[22] Scott's military secretary, Erasmus D. Keyes, stated that by the end of the Mexican campaign the general had an "almost idolatrous fancy for Lee, whose military genius he estimated far above that of any other officer in the army."[23]

As for Lee, he gained a great deal from the Mexican War. First came a hero's mantle. Repeatedly under fire, almost captured, risking his life on more than one occasion, Lee had performed in outstanding fashion. He emerged from the war with three brevet promotions to the rank of colonel. At the same time, he learned much about war from one of its greatest artists. Winfield Scott taught Lee that a small force, effectively led, can always defeat a numerically stronger foe. The tactical value of turning and flanking maneuvers, the necessity on occasion to abandon one's communication lines, the defensive strength of earthworks—all were lessons that Lee acquired from the man he most admired: General Scott. Lee also recognized the value of reconnaissance and aggressiveness. The good general takes great risks in the difficult pursuit of victory.

The Mexican War likewise pointed out to Lee that the successful general picks good subordinates, tells them what he wants on the eve of battle, and insures that the army is in proper position when the fighting begins. This makes it unnecessary for the commander to lead the attack himself. From the contest in Mexico, Lee's brilliant mind was much in evidence, as was his temperament for high command.

In six months of action in the field Robert E. Lee had demonstrated to all concerned that he was an extraordinary soldier. Yet he found little glory in war. In the middle of the Mexican War, Lee wrote his son Custis: "You have no idea what a horrible sight a battlefield is."[24]

Nation Versus Country

LEE RETURNED TO THE UNITED STATES AS A HERO AND WITH THE BREVET (TEMPORARY) rank of colonel. Yet when the army geared down from war, he resumed the familiar army routine of engineering work. Lee's first postwar tour was to Florida to inspect the coastal defenses. In April 1849, he received orders to proceed to Baltimore, Maryland, to take charge of the construction of Fort Carroll on the Patapsco River.

The driving of piles and laying of stones was tedious, but the three years in Baltimore were happy times for Lee. His family was with him. He could enjoy the pleasures of being a father in residence. Robert Jr. recalled much later: "At forty-five years of age he was active, strong and as handsome as he had ever been. . . . He was always bright and gay with us little folk, romping, playing and joking with us. . . . Although he was so joyous and familiar with us, he was very firm on all proper occasions, never indulged us in anything that was not good for us, and exacted the most implicit obedience. I always knew that it was impossible to disobey my father."[1]

Above: Lee in 1851-1852 when he was a lieutenant colonel in the army.

In May 1852, Lee received an appointment that was a plum in the U.S. Army: He was to become the ninth superintendent of the U.S. Military Academy. The position carried much prestige, in and out of the army. Lee would be head of a large command and the center of upstate New York society. The superintendent's home was a mansion compared to the post housing that Lee had known. On a personal note Lee's oldest son, Custis, was already a cadet there.

Lee asked the War Department to reconsider the appointment. He felt unqualified for so high an academic office. The War Department stood firm. In August, Lee and his family moved to West Point, New York.

Lee did not know that he had performed his last engineering work for the United States.

The academy was bigger and better than Lee remembered from fifteen years earlier. As a result, his daily routine was a tedious one of heavy correspondence, keeping records, making estimates of goods needed and moneys spent. Every document pertaining to the Military Academy crossed Lee's desk for approval. This even included a request that cadets be allowed to receive socks from home.[2]

What brought the greatest pressure on Superintendent Lee was his own conscience. He considered himself personally responsible for the physical health and moral well-being of every cadet. Worry over cadets falling behind in

Below: **The U.S. Military Academy as it looked in the 1850s, when Lee was stationed there.**

their studies filled many hours, and he wrote long letters to their parents in an effort to seek additional help. Lee took great pride in his son Custis, who graduated at the head of the class of 1854. However, others gave him deep concern.

One was his nephew Fitzhugh, son of Lee's beloved brother Smith Lee. Twice the young man came close to dismissal. Another cadet, named "Curly" Whistler, stood first in the subject of drawing but gave little attention to his other studies. Lee finally had to dismiss him from West Point. The former cadet became famous as the artist James McNeill Whistler, whose portrait of his mother is one of the best-known works in American art.

When a cadet was going to be expelled, Lee always gave him the opportunity to resign. To the father of one, Lee wrote: "He is a youth of such fine feelings and good character that I should not like to subject him to the mortification of failure, to which he might give more value than it deserves. For I consider the character of no man affected by want of success provided he has made an honest effort to succeed."[3]

Lee took no pleasure in disciplining students. Yet he believed "when it is necessary, true kindness requires it should be applied with a firm hand."[4]

A major change occurred in Lee during the West Point years. He came to feel a deeper sense of dependence on God. As a child he had been baptized in the Episcopal Church. He had never undergone confirmation as a member of

Above: **A formal portrait of Superintendent Lee at West Point. Although the position carried much prestige, Lee never enjoyed his duties.**

that faith. When danger came close to Lee in Mexico, so did God's presence.

In July 1853, Lee was confirmed into the Episcopal faith. The bishop who performed the ceremony said to him: "Colonel Lee, if you make as valiant a soldier for Christ as you have made for your country, the Church will be as proud of you as your country now is."[5] Thereafter, religion became a dominant presence in Lee's life.

His reputation for ability and heroism remained high in the War Department. By 1855 authorities knew that Lee was restless at West Point. Congress authorized the creation of two new regiments of infantry and two of cavalry. The Army Corps of Engineers was still Lee's first love. Although he held the temporary rank of colonel in the corps, he was but a captain on the army's active roster. Lee was aware that he had a better chance for promotion with cavalry rather than engineers. Duty in the field was far more appealing than sitting behind a desk.

The War Department was willing to assign Lee to the 2nd U.S. Cavalry. However, a dispute erupted between Secretary of War Jefferson Davis and General in Chief Winfield Scott. Davis wanted an old friend, Albert Sidney Johnston, appointed colonel of the regiment, with Lee to be second in command.

Scott pushed for Lee to lead the regiment. At one point Scott angrily told a friend: "If I were on my death-bed tomorrow, and the President of the United States should tell me that a great battle was to be fought for the liberty or slavery of the country, and asked my judgment as to the ability of a commander, I would say with my dying breath, let it be Robert Lee."[6]

The power of the secretary of war prevailed. Sidney Johnston became colonel of the 2nd Cavalry. Lee became second in command but received a double promotion to lieutenant colonel.

Three years at West Point had been good for Lee. He had made friends with men of influence, including former president Martin Van Buren, Gouverneur Kemble, and George Bancroft. Academic life at the school afforded Lee the opportunity to read more books than at any other time of his life. West Point expanded his horizon in both friendships and knowledge. In addition, Lee came to know prospective officers whom he later would command—as well as younger officers against whom he would fight.

On the last day of March 1855, Lee departed West Point. He was reluctant to leave his family again, especially the four daughters who needed the presence of a father. Yet army duty overrode family needs. Lee journeyed to Louisville, Kentucky, where the 2nd Cavalry was being formed. It would become an outstanding unit because it was so splendidly led. Both Colonel Johnston and Lieutenant Colonel Lee would become Confederate generals;

Opposite: **General in Chief of the Armies Winfield Scott (1786-1857) looked on Lee almost as a son and considered him one of the finest soldiers America had produced.**

Major George H. Thomas later rose to high prominence as a Union general; among the younger officers were John B. Hood, Earl Van Dorn, and E. Kirby Smith, all of whom were destined for a Southern general's stars.

From Louisville, the regiment proceeded to duty along the Texas frontier. Indian threats were constant; bandit raids occurred regularly. Virtually all of the army units were under-strength. A 1,000-man regiment only occasionally exceeded 400 men. The 2nd Cavalry was still recruiting when it entered field service.

Army life on the frontier was dull. It was a drab contrast to the intellectual and social atmosphere of West Point. Separation from family brought deep homesickness. Living conditions were terrible. Other than a forty-day march in pursuit of some Indians who had been stealing cattle, Lee spent the better part of two years fighting the greater enemies: disease, poor food, and exposure to the elements.

Such obstacles did not cloud his dedication to duty or his warm personality. A fellow officer stationed with Lee at an outpost near Abilene noted: "He examined everything thoroughly and continuously, until master of every detail, ever too conscientious to act under imperfect knowledge of any subject submitted to him. And with all his stern sense of duty, he attracted the love, admiration, and confidence of all. The little children always hailed his approach with glee—his sincerity, kindliness of nature, and cordial manners attracting their unreserved confidence."[7]

A loss in the family took Lee away from life on the frontier. His mother-in-law, Mary Fitzhugh Custis, had died when the Lees were at West Point. In October 1857, Mr. Custis passed away at Arlington. Mary Lee now inherited the debt-ridden Custis estates. Lee's two eldest sons, Custis and W. H. F. ("Rooney"), were both army officers at distant posts and thus unavailable to come to their mother's aid. Lee himself applied for an extended leave of absence to return to Virginia and take charge of family business. The War Department promptly gave permission.

What followed was a period of drudgery and a firsthand look at slavery. Mr. Custis had spent more time in good living than in good business. The plantation at Arlington was disorganized and run-down. Even worse for Lee, he found his forty-nine-year-old wife alone and in great pain. Mary had become so crippled by arthritis that she was virtually an invalid.

To repay debts and repair neglected Arlington was going to take much time and effort. Lee had to make repeated requests for extension of his furlough. For two years he labored dutifully in the life of a planter as he sought to restore his wife's home to its former condition. Lee's work was somewhat a race with time. Mr. Custis had made provision in his will for the emancipation of his sixty-three slaves within five years of his death.

Lee eventually freed them all. He allowed those who wished to remain at Arlington to do so. Lee set aside wages, should the ex-slaves wish to leave someday. Lee's kindness

Above: George Washington Parke Custis
(1781-1857) was Lee's father-in-law as
well as the adopted son of George Washington.
Custis's mismanagement of Arlington Estate
left the home briefly in shambles.

Right: Arlington Estate was the show place of the Washington-Alexandria area of the Potomac River. Mrs. Robert E. Lee inherited the home in 1857. Her husband lived there for most of the four years immediately prior to the Civil War.

reflected his feelings on the slave issue. In 1856 he had written to his wife: "In this enlightened age there are few, I believe, but what will acknowledge that slavery, as an institution, is a moral and political evil."[8]

Years as a slaveholding farmer at Arlington turned Lee against the system for practical reasons as well. Supporting families from birth to death in order to have a workforce did not strike Lee as efficient. Yet like most Southerners of his day, Lee had no solution to how slavery could survive in a free society. For Lee, slavery would end when God wanted it to end. "How long their subjugation may be necessary is known & ordered by a wise Merciful Providence. Their emancipation will sooner result from the mild & melting influence of Christianity, than [from] the storms and tempests of fiery Controversy."[9] In other words, Lee thought, politicians should cease their endless, fiery oratory and place the future of slavery in the all-powerful hands of God.

Whatever feelings Lee had about political issues and refurbishing Arlington ceased for the moment in October 1859. A terrorist raid occurred only fifty miles up the Potomac River from Lee's home. John Brown, a fifty-nine-year-

Right: When abolitionist John Brown (1800-1859) and twenty-two followers illegally seized the federal arsenal at Harpers Ferry, Virginia, Colonel Lee led the troops who ended the insurrection.

old abolitionist murderer, led some twenty followers in an attack on the huge U.S. arsenal at Harpers Ferry. Brown's plan was to seize arms while calling on all slaves in the region to rise up against their masters. Then Brown would lead a great exodus to freedom with whatever bloodshed might be required.

Brown captured the arsenal. Over the next twenty-four hours he and his men killed four townspeople, including a free black man. They also took a number of hostages. When word of the raid arrived in Washington, the War Department ordered Lee to restore order at Harpers Ferry. The only troops available were ninety men from the U.S. Marines. Lee did not pause to put on his colonel's uniform. In civilian dress he led the marines to Harpers Ferry. They stormed the fire-engine house where Brown and his men were barricaded. Several raiders were killed; others were captured. Brown himself was injured and taken prisoner.

Lee's report of the "John Brown Raid" was brief because the poorly led campaign had been squashed by the marines in three minutes. Lee termed the lawbreakers as nothing more than "rioters." The whole plan, he stated, "was the attempt of a fanatic or a madman, which could only end in failure."[10] Lee returned to Arlington unaware that the first shots of approaching civil war had been fired—and on Virginia soil.

Brown, quickly convicted of murder and treason, was sentenced to die. Northern abolitionists were angry over the impending "martyrdom" of one of their champions. Lee

received orders to return to the Harpers Ferry area with four companies of soldiers to block any illegal outbursts that might occur. On December 2, 1859, John Brown was hanged near the county courthouse in Charles Town. No incidents disrupted the execution.

By the end of the year Arlington was prospering again. Structures had been rebuilt, fields replanted, herds replenished. In February 1860, Lee returned to army duty at San Antonio, Texas. For a time he acted as commander of the Department of Texas. An Indian disturbance or border bandit occasionally brought trouble. Yet Lee increasingly faced a greater trouble: an ever-heating dispute among Americans over the issue of slavery.

The storm had been brewing for years. Now it had reached Texas. Most Southerners argued that since the Constitution recognized slavery, the practice of bondage was legal. Others maintained that because slavery was so obviously evil, the Constitution should be either ignored or changed. Southern extremists took refuge behind the Constitution; Northern extremists wanted action and new laws.

Heating the atmosphere even more was an ongoing feud over the nature of the American government. Most Northern leaders felt that sovereignty—ultimate power—rested with federal authorities. Most Southern spokesmen argued that since states existed before a nation, the rights of the states were supreme. Throughout 1860, Southern politicians and editors loudly advocated that their states should secede—leave the Union—and establish a government of their own to protect their way of life. Secession, they insisted, was the true alternative to both Northern agitation and war.

Lee became anxious over the future of a nation to which he had given thirty years of his life as a soldier. He watched the 1860 presidential election run its controversial course. The election of the all-Northern Republican candidate, Abraham Lincoln, led within weeks to movements for secession by a number of Southern states.

Colonel Lee was helpless to stop the political storm. A month after Lincoln's election Lee wrote his son Custis: "My only hope [is] for the preservation of the Union, and I will cling to it to the last. Feeling the aggressions of the North, resenting their denial of the equal rights of our citizens . . . I am [also] not pleased with the course of the 'Cotton States,' as they term themselves, [with their] selfish, dictatorial bearing. . . . While I wish to do what is right, I am unwilling to do what is wrong, either at the bidding of the South or the North."[11]

By mid-January 1861, five Southern states had left the Union. In a letter filled with anguish Lee revealed that he had already made up his mind about the future should it bring civil war. "I can anticipate no greater calamity for the country than a dissolution of the Union. . . . I am willing to sacrifice everything but honor for its preservation. . . . Secession is nothing but revolution. . . . A Union that can only be maintained by swords and bayonets, and in which strife and civil war are to take the place of brotherly love and kindness, has no charm for me."[12]

He had seen war and hated its destruction. Should the United States cease to be united, he would leave the army and return to Virginia. The land of his ancestors was his homeland, his birthright. The course of Virginia would be his course.

Other melancholy feelings plagued Lee in those first months of 1861. He was homesick. An invalid wife and four unmarried daughters were far away at Arlington. He was now fifty-three and only a lieutenant colonel. Since promotion in the army was based almost totally on seniority, and since twenty-two other colonels outranked him in date of appointment, the chances of Lee becoming a general were slim indeed. Lee did not know how to advance his cause. He was too modest a man to do so. His career was at a standstill while his country was falling to pieces.

Suddenly, in February, Lee received orders to proceed at once to Washington, D.C. No explanation was given. In the three weeks it took him to travel to the national capital, Lee must have thought of all the possible reasons he was being summoned to headquarters. On March 1 he and his army mentor, General in Chief Scott, had a private, three-hour meeting. No record exists of what they discussed. In all likelihood, Scott wanted his favorite officer nearby in case the secession crisis developed into war. Perhaps he told Lee that a quick promotion might be at hand if Scott found himself unable to take the field at the head of the U.S. Army.

Above: Pennsylvania Avenue was the
main street of Washington, D.C., in 1861.
Note the unfinished dome of the U.S.
Capitol on the eve of the Civil War.

By then Scott was a mountain of a man crumbled by age. He was 6 feet, 4 inches tall, weighed 300 pounds, and could not walk even a short distance without great effort. The hero of two wars was still the nation's foremost military figure since the sainted George Washington. Scott had served a half century in the army. Age and infirmity had now caught up with him.

Lee returned to Arlington from the meeting with Scott. In the days ahead, anxiety led to despair. Seven Southern states organized the Confederate States of America. The new government insisted that all national forts within its territory be transferred to the Confederacy. President Lincoln refused. The Union leader soon announced his intentions to send food supplies (not weapons) to the Federal garrison trapped at Fort Sumter, in the harbor of Charleston, South Carolina. Confederates responded by bombarding Fort Sumter. For thirty-six hours shells rained into and against the fort. The small Union garrison surrendered.

Gunfire had changed secession into war. On April 15, Lincoln issued a call on all states to furnish 75,000 troops to move against "combinations too powerful to be suppressed by the ordinary course of judicial proceedings."[13] This proclamation by Lincoln sent Virginia and three other states out of the Union and into the Confederacy.

Since February a state secession convention had been in daily session at Richmond. Delegates had argued over various aspects of slavery, but they were united in one line of thinking: Ultimate power in America lay with the states. Hence,

Federal troops could not exhibit coercion by marching across a state without that state's permission. Thus, when Lincoln called for troops to do precisely that, the Virginia Convention on April 17 voted overwhelmingly to leave the Union in order to protect what it regarded as its basic rights.

That same day, at Arlington, Lee received two messages. One was to call on Francis P. Blair Sr., an old friend and one of the most prominent public figures in Washington. The other note was an informal order to report to General Scott.

On the morning of April 18, Lee rode alone to the Blair home.[14] The seventy-year-old Blair greeted him warmly, then came straight to the point. A large Union army, Blair declared, was to be raised to enforce national laws in the rebellious South. The president of the United States had authorized Blair to ask Lee if he would take command of that great host.

Lee paused for a second. Here was everything he had spent a life trying to gain: command of an army, a general's rank, the full support of the government, many of his army friends working closely with him, the opportunity to apply all the lessons of war he had learned in Mexico. The offer was a dream come true. Yet Lee gave it only a passing thought.

For 225 years Lees had inhabited Virginia. The Old Dominion was 180 years old when the United States was created. Now Lincoln proposed to send soldiers into Virginia to enforce laws contrary to the dominant thinking in his state and its Southern sisters. Lee gave this simple account of his reply to Blair: "I declined the offer he made me to take command of the army that was to be brought into the field, stating as candidly and courteously as I could, that though opposed to secession and deprecating war, I could take no part in an invasion of the Southern States."[15]

Lee went from Blair's home to Scott's office a few blocks away. The old soldier welcomed Lee solemnly, for Scott doubtless knew of the offer that had been made. Lee told Scott what had happened. The general shook his head. "Lee," he said with emotion, "you have made the greatest mistake of your life; but I feared it would be so."[16]

Scott then expressed the belief that Lee should resign from the army as soon as possible. "There are times," he said, "when every officer in the United States service should fully determine what course he will pursue and frankly declare it."[17] Information might come, Scott added, that Lee ought not to hear or orders that Lee could not in his heart obey.

The next days brought the news that Virginia in fact had seceded. Duty to homeland now beckoned. On April 20, Lee submitted his resignation from the U.S. Army. As much as he loved the Union, he loved Virginia more. "I cannot raise my hand against my birthplace, my home, my children," Lee said.[18]

Lee's action was firm but reluctant. He was not caught up in the excitement of war, nor was he anxious to make a mark in the new turn of events. He felt heartache, resentment, certainly a tinge of anger, that North and South had brought the Union to war against itself. His

friends would be fighting on opposite sides. Lee himself prayed to avoid personal involvement in such a situation.

That was a forlorn hope. After attending church on Sunday morning, Lee received a request to meet with Virginia's governor, John Letcher, in Richmond. Lee knew what was taking place. He was going to be asked to participate in the defense of Virginia. The very reason he had resigned from the army—his allegiance to his beloved state—was now to be put to a more positive use. Lee met with Letcher, who wasted no time in offering Lee "command of the military and naval forces of Virginia," with the rank of major general.[19]

His native state needed him. His devotion to Virginia was total. On Tuesday afternoon, April 23, 1861, Lee appeared in civilian dress before the Virginia Convention. Thunderous applause greeted his introduction as the man now in charge of Virginia's military forces—and its future. Lee acknowledged the welcome with silent nods. Then, in the first speech of his life, he stated:

"Mr. President and Gentlemen of the Convention— Profoundly impressed with the solemnity of the occasion, for which I must say I was not prepared, I accept the position assigned me by your partiality. I would have much preferred had your choice fallen on an abler man. Trusting in Almighty God, an approving conscience, and the aid of my fellow-citizens, I devote myself to the service of my native State, in whose behalf alone will I ever again draw my sword."[20]

Lee now faced a civil war.

Rocky Path to Army Command

3

"General Lee, son of Light Horse Harry Lee, has been made general in chief of Virginia. With such men to the fore, we have hope."[1]

MARY BOYKIN CHESNUT, WIFE OF AN INFLUENTIAL SOUTH CAROLINA POLITICIAN, THUS MADE the first reference to Lee in the thick diary she would keep during the war years. Dozens of Lee references would follow throughout the journal.

Everyone agreed that Governor Letcher had chosen well. Lee looked like a general in chief. Now fifty-four years old, he still was taller and heavier than most men of his day. Lee was sound of body, not having been seriously ill in his entire life. Though his black hair was beginning to show sprinkles of gray, a short mustache was wholly black. He had the brown eyes and ruddy complexion of a Lee. His figure remained trim from riding, dancing, swimming, and athletic contests. Lee had even competed with his sons in high jumping when he was in his forties. Sitting behind a desk or riding a horse, his broad shoulders and thick frame made him appear larger than he actually was. The most pronounced contrast to the rest of the man were his extremely small feet. He wore a size 4½ shoe.[2]

In the spring of 1861, Lee was at the height of his intellectual powers. Always quick to learn

and balanced in judgment, he now had at hand a fund of knowledge and experience acquired through three decades in the army. He was a man of action, not of books. Even before acquiring a new uniform, General Lee established an office in the Richmond post office building and secured room and board at a nearby hotel.

Richmond was then a city of 38,000 citizens—the third-largest city in the South and the fastest-growing urban area below the Potomac River. Businesses and homes spread over the seven hills of Virginia's capital city. One-third of the population was black. That proportion dropped steadily after May 1861, when Richmond became the capital of the Confederate States as well. Government workers, office seekers, soldiers, and refugees would eventually swell the population to more than 100,000 people.

Virginia's principal town was heavily industrial. It was the closest thing to a manufacturing center that existed in the South. For that reason alone, Richmond had to be defended to the end. Yet the city was not Lee's major problem.

Amid the initial chaos of war he had to prepare the entire state of Virginia for conflict. That was no easy task. Virginia was the largest of the Confederate states. At the time it extended 425 miles from the Atlantic Ocean to the Ohio River. The state's 67,200 square miles made Virginia roughly the size of all of New England. With 1.5 million residents, the Old Dominion was also the most populous Southern state.

Lee's homeland contained a coastal area, rolling hills, and imposing mountains. Roads were numerous. Although the railroad had existed for only thirty years, Virginia had 1,150 miles of rail lines stretching to every corner of the state. Norfolk was a great harbor. Richmond contained everything from iron foundries to arsenals. The piedmont was the center of the wealthy tobacco trade. Orchards and fields in the Shenandoah Valley would make that region the "Bread Basket of the Confederacy." In mountainous southwest Virginia were vital coal deposits, lead mines, and saltworks. All of this had to be protected, and Lee was the man in charge of it.

Time was an enemy, for Union forces were marshaling all along the Potomac River line for invasions into Virginia. Behind the blue-clad soldiers were four times the population of the South. The North controlled 85 percent of the nation's factories, 67 percent of its acreage, 66 percent of its railroad mileage—and that was just the beginning of Northern superiority for making war.

Lee undertook his new duties with three goals in mind: to prepare defenses as quickly as possible; to secure as many weapons as were available; and to convince Virginians somehow that dedication and utmost sacrifice not only lay ahead, but were necessary for ultimate victory. Unlike most Americans, Lee did not view the Civil War as a small, one-battle, six-month affair. "Northern politicians do not appreciate the determination and pluck of the South," he said, "and Southern politicians do not appreciate the numbers, resources and patent perseverance of the North. Both sides forget that we are all Americans, and that it must be a terrible struggle."[3]

Lee confided to his wife in 1861 that he thought the war might last ten years. Regardless of the length, Lee faced the unknown with the same prayer: "In God alone must be our trust."[4]

A fairly well-developed militia existed in Virginia. It became the basis for the mobilization of state forces that Lee oversaw. Cadets from the Virginia Military Institute provided instruction in drill and basic army skills. Thousands of recruits flooded into the state. Organizing and equipping them required constant labor. Firebrands such as ex-governor Henry A. Wise and secessionist leader Edmund Ruffin urged that a Virginia force launch an invasion before the North could become fully prepared. Lee wisely chose to put the troops on the defensive

in order to gain as much time as possible for the big war to come.

The general worked daily with a combination of calm experience and great energy. He dispatched troops to the important military points: Norfolk and its valuable navy yard, the Shenandoah Valley avenue into both North and South, Manassas Junction and control of the two most important rail lines in northern Virginia. Construction of fortifications began on the three great rivers in the state: the James, York, and Rappahannock. Entrenchments soon encircled Richmond and other cities in the paths of possible attack.

Above: Richmond, Virginia, as it appeared during the Civil War years. Above the building with the blank wall, the state capitol is visible in the distance. The population in Richmond jumped from 38,000 residents in 1861 to more than 300,000 by 1865.

Above: George Washington Custis Lee (1832-1913), the oldest son of General Lee, spent most of the Civil War on engineering duties behind the lines. He succeeded his father as president of what is now called Washington and Lee University.

Next came the creation of a roster of officers and an efficient staff system. Lee assigned men to such branches as adjutant general, quartermaster, medical, and field duty. He obtained commissions for Virginians who had resigned from the U.S. Army and wanted to serve the Confederacy. Among the high-ranking appointments were Joseph E. Johnston, John B. Magruder, and Richard S. Ewell.

All three of Lee's sons became officers. Custis rose to the rank of major general of infantry. William Henry Fitzhugh rose to major general of cavalry. Young Robert Jr. enlisted as a private and ultimately became a captain of artillery.

All the while, Lee steadily built a defensive fighting force. He had thousands of men formed into units and fully armed in a month. Other regiments were training at hastily constructed army camps. Light artillery batteries came into existence, with shells seized from federal installations at Harpers Ferry and Norfolk. In all, Lee organized and equipped 60 regiments of infantry totaling about 50,000 men.

Captain Walter H. Taylor, a Norfolk businessman who would remain on Lee's staff throughout the war, marveled at the general's work habits. "I have never known a man more thorough and painstaking in all that he undertook," Taylor wrote. "Early at his office, punctual on meeting all engagements, methodical to an extreme in his way of dispatching business, giving close attention to details, but not . . . neglectful of the more important matters . . . he addressed himself to the accomplishment of every task . . . as if he himself was directly accountable to some higher power for the manner in which he performed his duty. He was not satisfied unless at the close of his office hours every matter requiring prompt attention had been disposed of."[5]

Lee's efforts brought him promotion from the Confederate Congress in late May to the rank of full general. He became the third highest ranking officer in the Confederacy, behind Albert Sidney Johnston and Adjutant General Samuel Cooper.

Scarcely had Lee completed the first mobilization when, on June 8, Virginia troops became part of the Confederate forces. In seven weeks Lee had mobilized, organized, trained, and deployed a sizable army to defend the Old Dominion. Richmond during that period became the capital of the Confederate States. Not one criticism was made of the defenses of either the city or the state.

President Jefferson Davis appointed Lee to the position of confidential military adviser. Lee was not at Manassas when the first major battle of the war was fought in July. Yet in a sense he was the hero of that contest, for he had selected the rail junction as a point of concentration and he had pulled together the forces that repulsed the first invasion of Virginia.

A week after the battle Lee received his first field command. Davis directed him to go to western Virginia, where other Union forces were making serious threats. A strong enemy column had advanced southward from the Baltimore and Ohio Railroad. On July 11 it had beaten a few thousand green Confederates at Rich Mountain. The Confederate commander, Robert S. Garnett, was killed in the action. Federals seized Cheat Mountain, a strongpoint overlooking the Parkersburg-Staunton turnpike. Now Union soldiers could easily march east to Staunton, a railhead and the principal city in the upper (southern) end of the Shenandoah Valley.

General William W. Loring had succeeded the fallen Garnett. He held the mountain passes around Huntersville. Eighty miles to the southwest, in the strategic Kanawha Valley corridor, small Confederate forces under Generals Henry Wise and John B. Floyd seemed unable to contain a second Union probe. Lee departed for western Virginia with no official orders. It seems Davis assumed that Lee's title and prestige would carry sufficient authority. His role was to be an adviser more than a leader.

That would not work, Lee quickly discovered. He found Loring's headquarters in Huntersville, a village crowded with sick soldiers and, in the words of a Confederate chaplain, "a most wretched and filthy town."[6] The first obstacle he encountered was Loring. The one-armed soldier was younger than Lee but had been an active Indian fighter when Lee was only a staff officer. Loring resented the "intrusion" of Lee into his territory.

Moreover, conditions in the region were dismal. The terrain was mountainous, the roads were all but impassable because of heavy rains, and the population overwhelmingly supported

Above: Confederate President Jefferson Davis (1808-1889) had Lee as a military adviser until appointing him in June 1862 to command the South's most important army.

the Union. Lee soon learned too that all three Confederate armies were demoralized, ill-equipped, and suffering from epidemics of such diseases as measles.

The presidential adviser took the initiative when it was obvious that Loring had no inclination to fight. Lee planned to bring several Confederate columns to bear against Federals entrenched at Rich Mountain. Loring gave but grudging cooperation to the offensive. It rained for twenty consecutive days. A downpour on the night of September 11–12 paralyzed Lee's command in a sea of mud and blocked a morning attack. (One Confederate swore that he saw "dead mules lying in the road, with nothing but their ears showing above the mud.")[7]

Lee's strategy was a complicated plan involving the movement of no less than five converging columns. Weather, plus poor leadership and inexperience in the ranks, led to resounding defeat before an attack in force could be made. A surgeon wrote of the attempts to march: "It was no uncommon thing for a mule to slide twenty feet down a slope, and I could see strong men sink exhausted trying to get up the mountain side."[8]

In despair, Lee decided to shift fronts. He ordered Loring with most of his command to follow him to the Carnifex Ferry area, fifty-five miles to the southwest. There Floyd and Wise faced a Union column pushing east up the Kanawha Valley to threaten the Virginia and Tennessee Railroad at Lynchburg. If Lee could repulse these Federals, he might be able to drive

W.ES.
after
W.U.Washington

them back across the Ohio River. This would secure the western counties firmly to Virginia.

The president's military adviser certainly made a good first impression at Carnifex Ferry. A soldier in the 22nd Virginia thought Lee "a most perfect figure, straight without stiffness, full chest, trim build in every respect, decidedly the handsomest figure I ever saw . . . courteous and

Above: **This sketch of one of Floyd's artillery pieces in its position overlooking the Kanawha River shows the rough and steep nature of the terrain Lee was trying to secure.**

perfectly easy in his manners, and with the most remarkable faculty for keeping his own counsel I have ever known . . . answering all questions civilly, but with good care that no one shall find out more than he intends them to know."[9]

Lee immediately discovered controversy rather than concentration. Neither Wise nor Floyd was a professional soldier. Each was a former governor, vain, jealous, and totally uncooperative with the other. Lee's premier

biographer wrote: "All his life Lee had lived with gentle people. . . . In that atmosphere, he was expansive, cheerful, buoyant even, no matter what happened. . . . Now that he encountered surliness and jealousy, it repelled him, embarrassed him, and well-nigh bewildered him."[10]

To solve the problem, Lee had Wise recalled to Richmond—a move that brought loud criticism from Wise's political friends in the state and national governments. Loring's forces were soon at hand. Lee then moved to attack the main portion of General William S. Rosecrans's Union army.

Deplorable roads, lack of supplies, the incompetent Floyd, and the grumbling Loring all worked against Lee's assault plans. The general decided to take a strong position atop Sewell Mountain and invite a Union attack. Federals refused to take the bait. Rosecrans withdrew from the trap and moved against the weak Confederate garrison at Huntersville. Lee tried to give pursuit, but the lack of transportation vehicles, the wretched condition of the roads, plus thin and pitiful horses blocked his advance. Lee had no choice but to pull all of the troops back to a new defensive line. His first offensive campaign had ended in complete failure.

Probably no commander could have gained victory in the face of all of the obstacles that Lee faced. On the other hand, his unwillingness to issue firm orders and demand firm obedience cost him several missed opportunities. The kindness that would enrich his later years as an army leader worked strongly to his disadvantage in western Virginia. Later in the autumn some fifty western counties seceded

from Virginia and began a two-year journey toward becoming the state of West Virginia.

Newspaper editors in Richmond blasted Lee's poor performance. They called him "Evacuating Lee" and accused him of being too cautious to fight.[11] Lee made no public response. To his wife, he expressed hurt. "I am sorry," he wrote, that "the movements of the armies cannot keep pace with the expectations of the editors of papers."[12] He displayed unusual sarcasm in telling a friend: "We appointed all of our worst generals to command the armies, and all our best generals to edit the newspapers."[13]

He returned to Richmond with two new personal features. One was a horse he acquired: a large gray stallion Lee called Traveller, which became the most famous mount in Civil War history.[14] The other change was the result of weeks of frustration. Lee's black hair had become noticeably gray.

President Davis was aware of the public outcry about Lee. He, too, was disappointed in Lee's field efforts. Yet Davis knew that the general was a proven and brilliant army engineer. Lee had been back in Richmond only five days when Davis ordered him to Charleston, South Carolina, to strengthen the coastal defenses against a large Union fleet anchored just offshore. Lee departed Richmond by train with a single aide, Armistead L. Long.

For four months the presidential adviser examined and strengthened fortifications in the Charleston-Savannah area. Lee at first found the defenses inadequate, the residents indifferent.

Above: John B. Floyd
(1806-1863) was Virginia's
governor and James
Buchanan's secretary
of war. As a field commander,
he was a failure.

The hesitation Lee displayed in western Virginia disappeared. He promptly abandoned outlying, isolated works and concentrated on Fort Pulaski (where he had worked twenty years earlier), Fort Sumter, and similar established defenses.

Lee next exhibited his engineering skills by undertaking an elaborate overhaul of protective works for the miles of Carolina coasts. Some

12,300 Confederates scattered here, there, and everywhere were to concentrate where they were most needed. An interior line of heavy earthworks would be built to protect the rail line and other vital points. All able-bodied men—rich and poor, free and slave—were put to work digging entrenchments and filling sandbags.

Fortunately for Lee, the Union forces circling a mile or so out in the Atlantic Ocean made no move toward an offensive. The Confederate preparations continued without interruption. Lee's assignment was unexciting, the work was dull, complaints from unwilling laborers were loud. Yet the effort was essential to the Confederate cause. In the western theater the great fortress on the Mississippi River at Columbus, Kentucky, had been abandoned. General Sidney Johnston had evacuated most of Kentucky and half of Tennessee. Up the Atlantic coast, Roanoke Island had fallen into Union hands in February and was now a valuable jumping-off point for ships and men. Not since October 1861 had the South gained a military victory.

As always, Lee met these setbacks with his usual courage. He wrote home: "We must make up our minds to meet with reverses and to overcome them. I hope God will at last crown our efforts with success."[15] On March 2, Lee boasted of the Charleston defenses to his daughter Annie: "If our men will stand to their work, we shall give [the enemy] trouble and damage them yet."[16]

Lee's work on coastal fortifications ended that same day, when Davis asked him to return to Richmond. The four-month assignment had been both good and bad for Lee. Challenges were many, but work was drudgery. He had exerted independent command well but still showed some reluctance to be stern with stubborn subordinates. His strengthening of the defenses of Charleston and Savannah went far in preventing those cities from falling into Union hands until the final months of the war.

What he accomplished gave Lee new faith in the power and effectiveness of fieldworks. On the other hand, many who had toiled hard saw no need for the earthworks. The South surely would win the war on the battlefield, they asserted. So the critics gave Lee a new, uncomplimentary nickname: the "King of Spades."[17]

Virginia was in a desperate situation when Lee arrived back in Richmond. The Confederate government was showing dangerous weaknesses. Many of Jefferson Davis's early followers were now doubtful of his abilities. Army supplies were low. The one-year enlistment terms of thousands of soldiers would end in April. Two weeks after Lee's return the greatest army ever assembled on the American continent landed on the Virginia peninsula east of Richmond. Over 100,000 Union soldiers under Lee's fellow staff officer in Mexico, General George B. McClellan, intended to seize the capital. Such a conquest would end the Civil War.

No one suggested Lee as the man who could go into the field and block disaster. Instead, on March 13, Davis assigned Lee to "the seat of government . . . under the direction of the

President." Lee was to be in charge of "the conduct of military operations in the armies of the Confederacy."[18] His new position was roughly the same as today's army chief of staff.

The appointment gave Lee much responsibility but little power. He could issue commands to generals at the front, but he himself had no command. While he was flooded with details to handle, Lee was unable to initiate any plans of his own. "I cannot see either advantage or pleasure in my duties," he admitted privately.[19]

Others now saw him as just another paper-pusher, another babysitter for the armies. A new nickname sprang up overnight: "Granny Lee," a man too genteel and timid to do the dirty work of war.[20]

That did not stop Lee from performing his duties to the fullest. His advice to General Johnston in the western theater led to a concentration of Confederate forces and an April 6 attack on General Ulysses S. Grant's army at Shiloh. The offensive came close to a success. It failed for reasons beyond Lee's control.

One of Lee's most valuable contributions during this period was his strong support for conscription. The drafting of young men into the armies had never been done before in America. Lee was aware that professional armies were the tradition. He also knew that the outmanned South needed to give its fullest effort to the war. Because the basic duty of the Confederate nation was to wage war until independence was secured, Lee declared, "the whole nation should for a time be converted

into an army, the producers to feed and the soldiers to fight."[21] Such strong support helped to persuade the Confederate Congress later in April to pass an act for summoning men into the armies.

Conscription actually was a display of optimism on the part of the South. It was based on the assumption that the new nation was going to endure a long time. The military situation in the spring of 1862 gave a different picture.

The most urgent concern for Lee became the defense of Virginia. General George McClellan's massive Army of the Potomac had landed on the Virginia peninsula in and around Yorktown for a direct advance on Richmond. Union strategy was for the army to proceed west one hundred miles up the land flanked by the James and York rivers. The only expected opposition was the smaller force of General Joseph E. Johnston, posted somewhere near the capital.

Meanwhile, a second Union army under General Irvin McDowell was encamped at Fredericksburg. It could start a fifty-mile march south to Richmond at any time. If that happened, Richmond would be squeezed to death by overwhelming numbers approaching from two different directions.

Right: Although Lee and Thomas J. Jackson (1824-1863) hardly knew each other before the Civil War, they would form an almost model partnership on the battlefield. Legends would abound about Robert "Marse Robert" Lee and Thomas "Stonewall" Jackson.

Lee's first thought was to ask Johnston to march down the peninsula, assail McClellan hard enough to bring his advance to a halt, then turn back and move on McDowell to the north. That was unlikely to work, Lee concluded, because of Johnston himself. Lee's friend of many years had a hot temper. He resented anyone telling him what to do. Even worse, Lee's original plan called for daring and swiftness. Johnston did not possess either talent.

One thing was certain: The Confederates had to do something. To sit back and watch the approach of the Federals would be like a condemned man waiting for the executioner. Nor could the Confederates retreat to any advantage. At a cabinet meeting in mid-May, Lee dutifully mentioned one or two strategic alternatives. Suddenly, his real feelings emerged. "But Richmond must not be given up!" he exclaimed. "It shall not be given up!"[22]

Always believing that the best defense was an offense, Lee faced the question of how to make an attack that would disrupt the huge concentration of Union forces. The answer came from a Confederate force guarding the northern entrance to the Shenandoah Valley. It numbered only 3,000 men. Commanding this unit was a longtime Virginia Military Institute professor named Thomas J. Jackson.

He had graduated from West Point and been a hero in the Mexican War prior to winning the name "Stonewall" for a rocklike stand against Union forces in the victory at First Manassas. Jackson was strange to most people: silent, reserved, humorless, his every waking hour dedicated to the service of God. Convinced that a Confederate and a Christian were one and the same thing, Jackson wanted to fight this civil war as if it were a religious crusade.

Lee felt that if Jackson could be given a few reinforcements and turned loose on his own, he might be aggressive enough to at least disorganize Union military movements and at most threaten Washington itself. The two men began a constant contact by letter and telegram. They were not acquainted personally, and they were 120 miles apart, but Lee and Jackson thought alike. Each respected the other.

In April three small Union armies began moving into the Shenandoah Valley. Jackson was threatened from north, west, and east. The three Union generals facing Jackson were not close together. If Jackson could somehow defeat each one separately, Lee suggested, this might alarm Union officials sufficiently to stop McDowell from leaving Fredericksburg and proceeding toward Richmond. That in turn would leave McClellan alone and at the full attention of the Army of Northern Virginia.[23]

Lee's idea was daring, and it was risky. Practically everything depended on Jackson's speed and hard hitting. Jackson was more than willing to take the offensive. As McClellan's 100,000 troops inched toward Richmond, with Johnston seemingly preferring to give ground rather than give battle, Jackson behaved like anything but an immobile stone wall. He began a deadly game of hide-and-seek.

On May 9 he suddenly appeared in the mountains west of Staunton at the upper end of the Shenandoah Valley. A sharp fight with McDowell sent one of the three Union forces scurrying to safety. Jackson retraced his steps and picked up General Richard Ewell's reinforcing division along the way. The Confederates marched long and rapidly each day. Soon they had earned the title "foot cavalry" because they supposedly moved faster and farther than mounted soldiers could do.[24]

May 23 brought another battle victory at Front Royal at the other end of the Shenandoah. Two days later, in a resounding success at Winchester, Jackson sent Union soldiers of a second force into a wild retreat that carried them across the Potomac River. In Washington a frightened Union War Department ordered McDowell to forget his march south and to remain at Fredericksburg until further notice.

Lee could now breathe a little easier. A general he barely knew had appeared almost from nowhere and put the North into a defensive frame of mind. Stonewall Jackson brought victory at a time when the South most needed a boost in spirit. Jackson also gave Lee and Davis time to bring reinforcements to Johnston's command.

By late May, with rain falling daily, the two opposing armies faced each other barely five miles from Richmond. The long-expected battle for Richmond began on the last day of the month at a hamlet called Seven Pines. The Chickahominy River flowed diagonally across the peninsula. Heavy rains had sent the stream out of its banks. In doing so, it cut McClellan's army into two unconnected parts.

Johnston at first planned to attack north of the Chickahominy. Then he learned that McDowell was no longer a threat. The Confederate commander chose to assault the weaker Federal lines south of the river. Little went right for the Confederates that day. What should have been a pulverizing attack became a disjointed fight between two armed mobs.

One division went marching down the wrong road. Another division somehow never got into action. Those who fought had to battle floodlike conditions as well as the enemy. The ground won by Johnston's men in the first day's fighting was lost in the action of the second day.

President Davis and Lee rode onto the battlefield on June 1 in search of Johnston and news of the engagement. They found the general in the midst of confusion. Johnston was on a litter, too badly wounded to discuss either the battle or his plans for what would happen next. Johnston's second in command, General Gustavus Smith, had little knowledge of the situation—and apparently wanted none.

That Friday evening Lee and Davis rode dejectedly back to Richmond. Seated side by side on their horses, the two men discussed the day's events. Davis suddenly made the supreme decision of the Civil War. In the dark, on a muddy road, Robert E. Lee received command of the battered and disorganized Army of Northern Virginia. The future of Richmond and Virginia and the war now rested on his shoulders.

Brilliance in the Field

LEE KNEW FROM THE START THAT THE ARMY OF NORTHERN VIRGINIA WOULD EITHER WIN THE decisive victory in the Civil War or it would suffer the ultimate defeat of the Confederacy. Reactions to his appointment to field command were strongly mixed. The *Richmond Examiner* was openly critical. The army would never be allowed to fight, its editor wrote. It would just dig, "spades and shovels being the only implements Gen. Lee knew anything about."[1]

The Union's General McClellan was of the same frame of mind. He told Lincoln that while Lee was "personally brave and energetic to a fault, he yet is wanting in moral firmness when pressed by heavy responsibility and is likely to be timid and irresolute in action."[2]

Inside the Confederate army there was anything but confidence over the assignment of Lee. He was a skilled engineer, an excellent administrator, but untested in battle. Generals inside the army might quarrel with and dislike one another personally, but they would stand together against an "outsider" coming into their midst—especially if he was a new commander over them all. Down in the ranks the soldiers did not know enough about Lee to have an opinion.

At the other end of the scale the commander in chief trusted Lee. Davis's judgment was all that counted. Many years later Davis said of Lee at the time of the appointment: "Laborious and

exact in details, as he was vigilant and comprehensive in grand strategy, [he had] a power, with which the public had not credited him, [which] soon became manifest in all that makes an army a rapid, accurate, compact machine, with responsive motion in all its parts."[3]

Joseph C. Ives, a member of Davis's staff, was asked at the time if Lee had the dash and the personality to be an army chief. Ives replied: "If there is one man in either army . . . head and shoulders above every other in audacity, it is General Lee! His name might be Audacity. He will take more desperate chances and take them quicker than any other general in this country, North or South, and you will live to see it, too."[4]

The general took command painfully aware of the criticisms expressed of him. Lee turned a deaf ear. He possessed more than mere self-confidence. Behind him were thirty-four years of military experience. He had been in the U.S.

Above: General Lee as the commander of the Army of Northern Virginia. He rarely wore lavish uniforms and preferred a colonel's insignia (as George Washington had worn) to the ornate general's emblem.

Army long enough to know personally or by reputation most of the senior officers on both sides. Lee had the support of President Davis; and in contrast to the uncommunicative Joseph Johnston, Lee would go to great lengths to keep the president regularly informed of the situation in the field.

Lee had a remarkable ability to win the support of strongly differing subordinate officers. He never criticized in public; he accepted men as they were while always appealing to their highest impulses. For the common soldiers who filled his ranks, Lee would become half commander and half father.

One of his first acts after taking army command was to order better earthworks constructed around Richmond. Digging trenches was no work for gentlemen. Politicians and editors began using the old nickname for Lee: "King of Spades." Lee answered the remarks by declaring: "There is nothing so military as labor, and nothing so important to an army as to save the lives of its soldiers."[5]

Just as Lee was constantly concerned for soldiers' welfare, they became constant in the respect—and ultimately in the adoration—they had for him. Of all of the armies in the Civil War, none would maintain higher morale, in the face of more hardships, than the Army of Northern Virginia. The reason for this was one word: Lee.

From the moment he took command in the bloody wake of Seven Pines, Lee began thinking of a counterattack. His first idea was to leave a thin force to guard Richmond against the

snail-like movement of McClellan and rush heavy reinforcements to Jackson for a full-scale invasion of the North by way of the Shenandoah Valley. Lee discovered quickly that Confederate resources were not sufficient for such a long-distance offensive.

That led to an alternate strategy. Lee would have Jackson fake an invasion of the North. Such would hold McDowell in place at Fredericksburg. Lee could concentrate all of his forces for a major attack on McClellan. Jackson did more than carry out a feint. The Confederate general soundly thrashed two pursuing Union forces at Cross Keys (June 8) and Port Republic (June 9). In one of the most spectacular campaigns in modern history, Jackson had cleared the valley of all Union troops and totally immobilized any advance by McDowell.

Now it was Lee's turn to act. He dispatched his colorful cavalry chief, General James Ewell Brown "Jeb" Stuart, on a raid to determine the northernmost point of McClellan's army. Stuart was then twenty-nine, of medium height, with blue eyes, bushy brown beard, and heavy mustache. He wore a splendid uniform that included a yellow silk sash and an ostrich plume in his hat. Dashing and fun-loving, Stuart was courageous and lighthearted. That combination would not always serve him well.

At this point, however, Stuart achieved thrilling success. He not only obtained the information; for good measure, Stuart returned to Richmond by riding around the entire Union army at a cost of one casualty!

Above: **Creator and commander of the Union's Army of the Potomac, General George B. McClellan (1826-1885) was a skillful organizer and champion morale builder. Yet McClellan's caution in the field would prove his undoing.**

Meanwhile, Lee was carefully rebuilding the Army of Northern Virginia. Recruits eagerly filled gaps in the regiments. Officers came increasingly to be impressed by Lee's organizational skills, patience, and confidence. Surrounded for the most part by men he could trust, Lee now turned to the Union army poised at his front. McClellan had almost twice the infantry that Lee could muster. Confederate artillery was no match for Union cannons, which were larger in number and greater in accuracy. The Federal host was so close to Richmond that some Union pickets could set their watches by the chiming of the bells in Richmond churches.

Had McClellan pushed forward in full force, the Southern capital would have fallen. Instead, the uncertain Union commander believed he was heavily outnumbered! McClellan spent the first three weeks in June begging for more troops and finding excuses for not advancing the last few miles to Richmond.

McClellan's right flank stretched northward like a hand reaching for McDowell's force at Fredericksburg. The flank was uncovered, or "hanging in the air," Stuart's cavalry had discovered. Lee moved to take advantage of this weakness. His battle plan was a complicated one. Jackson's men would march quickly across Virginia and fight their way around McClellan's flank. Lee, with most of his army, would shift to the north side of the Chickahominy River and strike the Union flank from a different direction. A thin Confederate line in McClellan's

Opposite: **Lee's first offensive as an army commander was the June to July 1862 Seven Days' Campaign on the Virginia Peninsula to the east of Richmond. Note how close the Union army got to the Confederate capital.**

front would hopefully create enough noise and commotion to hold the Union general's attention.

Lee's strategy was bold as well as dangerous. He was seizing the initiative with a smaller force. By massing his troops on the enemy's extreme point, Lee was leaving his front—the main approach to Richmond—virtually unguarded. The Seven Days' campaign (June 26–July 1) was not what Lee wanted in the beginning. Yet the end result was a success.

Confederates hammered McClellan's army in a succession of battles at Mechanicsville, Gaines' Mill, Savage's Station, Glendale, and Malvern Hill. All the while, a totally unsettled McClellan led his army in retreat southward across the peninsula toward the safety of the James River and the large guns of a Federal fleet anchored there. Lee won the June 27 engagement at Gaines' Mill but failed to achieve victory in the other actions.

His July 1 blind infantry attacks against Union artillery massed atop Malvern Hill were

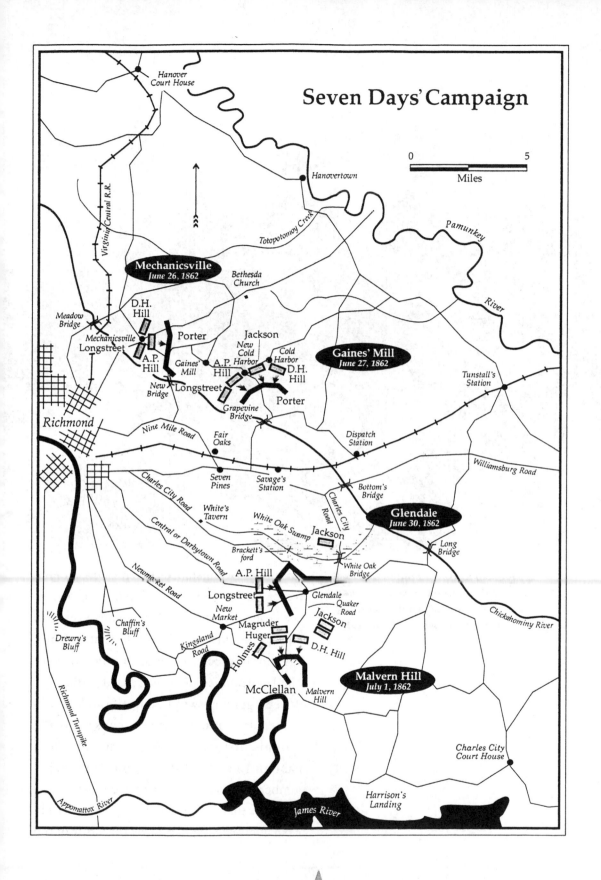

Seven Days' Campaign

0 — 5
Miles

Hanover Court House

Hanovertown

Pamunkey River

Totopotomoy Creek

Virginia Central R.R.

Mechanicsville
June 26, 1862

Bethesda Church

Meadow Bridge

D.H. Hill

Porter

Mechanicsville
Longstreet

A.P. Hill

Jackson

New Cold Harbor

Gaines' Mill

A.P. Hill

Cold Harbor

D.H. Hill

Gaines' Mill
June 27, 1862

Tunstall's Station

New Bridge

Longstreet

Grapevine Bridge

Porter

Richmond

Nine Mile Road

Fair Oaks

Dispatch Station

Williamsburg Road

Seven Pines

Savage's Station

Bottom's Bridge

Charles City Road

White's Tavern

White Oak Swamp

Jackson

Glendale
June 30, 1862

Central or Darbytown Road

Brackett's ford

Long Bridge

White Oak Bridge

Newmarket Road

A.P. Hill

Longstreet

Glendale

Quaker Road

Jackson

Chickahominy River

Chaffin's Bluff

New Market

Magruder

Drewry's Bluff

Kingsland Road

Huger

D.H. Hill

Holmes

Richmond Turnpike

McClellan

Malvern Hill

Malvern Hill
July 1, 1862

Charles City Court House

Appomattox River

Harrison's Landing

James River

Above: An artist sketched Lee and Jackson as the Confederate army was pursuing McClellan's retreating troops across the Peninsula.

the first of two instances when Lee's courage overcame his judgment. Each time one of Lee's cannons fired, fifty Union guns answered. The open-field assault by Confederate infantry was shot to pieces. Over 5,300 soldiers were killed or wounded in the one-sided battle. One of Lee's generals wrote sadly of the Malvern Hill repulse: "It was not war—it was murder."[6]

In his first undertaking as an army commander, Lee saved Richmond. However, a number of factors made the Seven Days' campaign less than a clear-cut victory. Lee failed in his major objective to destroy the Army of the

Potomac. His battle plan called for converging columns to move over unfamiliar roads at precise times. Inexperienced officers and green troops could not execute such maneuvers.

The key individual in the great turning movement was Jackson, who was too physically and mentally exhausted from the valley campaign to be even dependable on the peninsula. Lee's orders during the battles were few and unclear. None of his staff officers had the training or rank to insure that directives were obeyed fully.[7] Casualties in the week's fighting amounted to 20 percent of Lee's army. Confederate losses were more than twice those of the Union. Victory, produced at a cost of one of every five men, did not make the future look promising.

Such facts were not important at the time. Richmond had been saved. The Army of Northern Virginia had proven its worth in battle. McClellan had lost almost 10,000 men, as well as 52 cannons and 31,000 muskets. Union authorities abandoned the campaign up the peninsula. After Southern losses suffered from Roanoke Island, North Carolina, to New Orleans, Louisiana, Lee's electrifying success was a tremendous boost to Confederate morale. Overnight, "Granny Lee" had become a dazzling field general.

Lee himself was not excited at the outcome. He was grateful to God and to his army. Nevertheless, stopping McClellan did not mean the end of the war. Much more remained to be done if the Confederacy were to live.

The South always enjoyed one favorable position in the Civil War. It had no territorial ambitions; it did not want to occupy the North. The South simply wanted to be left alone. Therefore, and from a military standpoint, the South did not have to conquer the North. All it needed to do was make the war so expensive that the North would stop its resistance to Southern independence.

Davis and Lee disagreed over the basic strategy to follow with that outlook. The president wanted to defend every inch of the Confederacy. A major defeat in battle, Davis thought, would be the end of the Southern nation. To Lee, staying on the defensive merely postponed defeat. Time was not on the side of the Confederate States. The South's limited resources and manpower could not sustain a long war. Therefore, Lee wanted to seize the offensive and hopefully strike a blow so hard that the Northern will to continue the struggle would collapse.

With that difference in thought present, Lee used the lull after the Seven Days' campaign to reorganize his army. He got rid of some officers who did not meet standards he thought necessary for efficiency. Lee also selected two generals who would command the two wings of his army.

James Longstreet, a forty-one-year-old South Carolinian, was heavyset, ambitious, and very dependable when the army was on the defensive. "Old Pete" began the Civil War as a fun-loving, partygoing officer. However, in the winter of 1861–62, three of his children died in a scarlet fever epidemic in Richmond. After that he became a quiet, often sullen man. By late spring 1862 he was the ranking major general in the army. If Longstreet had "the slows," as some critics charged, he was as slow in giving ground as he was in gaining it.[8]

The other selection Lee made was Thomas "Stonewall" Jackson. Many considered it an odd choice. A thirty-seven-year-old orphan from the mountains of northwest Virginia, Jackson had won a great victory in the Shenandoah campaign but performed poorly in the Seven Days'. Jackson hardly looked inspiring. Although he was tall and strongly built, he wore a plain uniform and was a man of few words. Brown hair and beard surrounded large blue eyes that were difficult to see because his cap rested almost on his nose. Above all else, Jackson was a God-loving man. He fought for the Lord with the same blind obedience that he expected from every one of his soldiers.

No one would have faulted Lee for transferring Jackson elsewhere after the fighting around Richmond. Yet Lee knew a soldier when he saw one. He recognized in Jackson the instincts of a solid patriot. Jackson needed another chance to show his full capacities. Lee gave him that chance, and for the next eleven months the two Virginia generals would form an almost-perfect military partnership.

In mid-July the quietness of the war in Virginia disappeared. Lee received word that a second Union army was marching in the northern part of the state. At its head was General John Pope, a vain, self-confident officer who had achieved some success out west along the Mississippi River. Pope intended to use the line of the Orange and Alexandria Railroad through the rolling piedmont country of Virginia to get at Richmond. He boasted that his "headquarters would be in the saddle." This led Confederates to snort that Pope would be easy to whip because "he doesn't know his headquarters from his hindquarters."[9]

Lee displayed an amazing ability to anticipate what the enemy planned to do. Analyzing reports from several sources, Lee correctly believed that while McClellan's army was still huddled along the bank of the James River, it was not going to make another attempt at Richmond. Once again the Confederate commander would show extraordinary boldness. He determined to remain with half of the Southern army in front of Richmond. Jackson would march northward with the other half and delay Pope as long as possible. Lee would join Jackson as soon as the area around Richmond was empty of Federals.

On August 9, Jackson struck the lead elements of Pope's army at Cedar Mountain. The all-day fight south of Culpeper hung in the balance until the arrival of General A. P. Hill's large division turned the tide and brought a Confederate victory. Pope stopped his advance and assumed a defensive position inside the triangle formed by the junction of the Rappahannock and Rapidan rivers.

McClellan by then had begun leaving

Above: Casualties are a part of every battle. Here, Union soldiers are loading wounded men from wagons onto flat cars for rail transportation to an army hospital.

the peninsula. His orders were to return to Washington and reinforce Pope's efforts in the northern piedmont. Lee now rushed to unite with Jackson. Together they might be able to destroy Pope's force before McClellan's brigades started arriving. Pope got word of the Lee-Jackson reunion in his front. All of his boasting ceased. He began retiring with his army toward Washington.

On the night of August 23 cavalry chief Jeb

Above: This graphic illustration depicts a dead horse, wrecked equipment, plus wounded and weary soldiers along the path of Union General John Pope's army withdrawing from the Second Manassas battlefield.

Stuart raided Pope's headquarters at Catlett's Station. The Confederate general took Pope's dress uniform in an exchange for a hat Stuart had lost a couple of days earlier in a brief clash with Union cavalry. Stuart also seized some military papers that confirmed the pending junction of the armies of Pope and McClellan. Lee would have to act quickly and decisively if he expected a victory of any sort.

The next day Lee decided again to take a big gamble. Jackson would take one-third of the army and march northward toward Thoroughfare Gap in the Bull Run Mountains. The 23,000 Confederates were to use Jackson's best-known tactics: secrecy and speed. Once through Thoroughfare Gap, Jackson was to sweep around Pope's rear and destroy the Federal supply base at Manassas Junction. Lee would lead the rest of the army in a head-on pursuit of Pope.

His plan almost invited disaster. The general was dividing his forces in the face of superior numbers—a violation of one of the basic military principles of war. If Jackson encountered delays, or if Pope suddenly attacked the weakened Lee, the Army of Northern Virginia could be destroyed. However, Lee was confident of Pope's inertia and Jackson's skills.

What followed was one of the most celebrated marches in American history. As Lee waited anxiously Jackson led his "foot cavalry" fifty-six miles over the course of two days. Confederates struck the Orange and Alexandria Railroad at Bristoe Station, wrecked several trains, then marched through the night and seized Manassas Junction at daybreak. Tons of supplies were visible in every direction. For hungry, ill-clothed Confederates, it was Christmas in August. Jackson gave his men a day to take all of the stores they could carry. Then he set fire to the supply depot and slipped away.

Lee was thrilled. As Pope started northward to catch Jackson, Lee sent Longstreet's part of the army northward to bag Pope. Jackson had taken a defensive position that was partly behind the cut of an unfinished railroad. On August 28, Jackson's men attacked Pope's column at Groveton. The next day Pope unleashed assaults against Jackson's position.

Federals pounded the Confederate lines, but they could not break them. Ammunition began to run low in Jackson's front. When it did, members of a South Carolina brigade hurled rocks to stop a fresh attack. Jackson's stand enabled Longstreet and his troops to slip unnoticed in a position on the Union left flank. Lee's army was back together—with Pope's forces caught between the two wings.

On August 30, Pope renewed the head-on charges against Jackson's weakened lines. For hours the fighting raged as Jackson's men refused to give ground. Lee then gave a signal. Longstreet's forces suddenly slammed into the Union flank with the force of a tidal wave. Pope's army could not move because it was locked in combat with Jackson. Lee then signaled for both wings to advance and close on the now-confused Pope. By nightfall Federal columns were stumbling northward toward the defenses of Washington. In Richmond happy youngsters learned new words to a popular tune:

> Little Be-Pope, he came at a lope,
> The Rebels to find them.
> He found them at last, then ran very fast,
> With his gallant invaders behind him![10]

Jackson and others wanted to follow the beaten Union army into the Northern capital. Lee knew that it could not be done. Heavy rains began at the end of the battle of Second Manassas and turned the land into sticky mud. Some sixty-eight forts around the edges of Washington made it the strongest city in the Western Hemisphere. Lee's troops needed rest and food, while horses needed forage. Lee had to be content with a battle victory.

Second Manassas was a bloody campaign for both sides. Pope lost over 13,800 men—killed, wounded, or captured. Lee's casualties totaled 8,300 soldiers, many of them good officers he could not afford to lose. Still, it was this battle that placed Lee on a pedestal from which he never descended.

Lee had designed the movement and led his army on a daring offensive that stopped another Union drive on Richmond. The gray-haired commander had outwitted his opponent, out-maneuvered the enemy forces, and brought his army together at the moment when a crushing attack was most needed. A North Carolina brigadier proudly wrote his wife that Lee's army had "performed the most brilliant and daring feats of generalship and soldiership ever performed. The boldness of the plan and the quickness and completeness of execution were never beaten. Lee had immortalized himself and Jackson added new laurels to his brow."[11]

The victory at Second Manassas was military genius. Lee never thought so. He had a simple explanation for how he waged war. "I plan and work with all my might to bring the troops to the right place at the right time. With that I have done my duty. As soon as I order the troops forward into battle, I lay the fate of the army in the hands of God."[12]

Certainly, the campaign ended one of the greatest turnarounds in military history. Ninety days earlier, a massive Union army had driven to the outskirts of Richmond. Lee had taken command of the weak and disorganized Confederate army. He then defeated the enemy forces in front of Richmond, turned and defeated a second Union force approaching from another direction. By the end of August no enemy troops of note were in Virginia, and the capital in jeopardy was not Richmond but Washington. All of this had been accomplished through the strategy (planning) and tactics (movements) of Lee alone.

No time existed to bask in the sunlight of success, Lee knew. The war must be pressed anew. Northern forces were wounded, not dead. Another decisive blow must be delivered. That is why Lee concluded to carry the war to the enemy by invading the North.

The Bloodiest Day

SOME HISTORIANS CRITICIZE LEE FOR UNDERTAKING A CAMPAIGN THAT RESULTED IN THE single bloodiest day in American history. That is unfair. A person can always use clear hindsight to find fault with decisions made in unclear conditions. Actually, Lee's determination to strike into the North rested on good reasons and sound possibilities.

Union forces in the Virginia theater were demoralized. The state was clear of any Federal threat. A campaign somewhere else would allow Virginia farmers to gather what late-summer crops they had. Maryland was a slaveholding state, with many of its sons already in the Confederate army. A march into the state might bring Maryland into the Confederacy as well as a new rush of recruits into Lee's army.

Political and diplomatic considerations were also involved in Lee's thinking. Congressional elections would occur within two months. If Lee could win a stunning victory on Northern soil before then, war weariness might cause the North to elect men who would end the struggle. At the same time, both England and France seemed to be leaning in favor of granting official recognition to the Southern Confederacy. A major success by Lee on Union territory would surely convince one or both European nations to side with the South. That could bring supplies,

weapons, and possible manpower crashing through the Union naval blockade to the aid of the Confederates.

Lee had to face negative factors as well in reaching his decision. Limited supplies would not allow him to remain in the North for a long period. The Confederates would be conducting a raid, not a lengthy invasion. The strike would have to be quick and decisive. A second problem was that Lee's army was not in good shape to do either. Ranks were thin from battle losses in the several engagements of the past three months. Other Confederate soldiers felt that it was just as wrong for them to invade the North as it was for Billy Yanks to march into the South. Large numbers of Confederates drifted away and did not return to duty until the army was back in Virginia.

Even Lee admitted that the force he had at hand was weak. He told President Davis: "The army is not properly equipped for an invasion of the enemy's territory. It lacks much of the material of war, is feeble in transportation, the animals being much reduced, and the men are poorly provided with clothes, and in thousands of instances are destitute of shoes."[1]

While Lee was making these critical decisions, he also was suffering from the worst accident he had ever had. Lee was holding the reins of Traveller on the morning of August 31 when a sudden commotion frightened the animal. It reared and jerked Lee off-balance. The general instinctively stretched out both hands to cushion the fall, but he hit the ground hard. The fall broke one hand and badly sprained the other. Lee entered Maryland by riding in a carriage while holding his hands up to try to ease the pain.[2]

On September 5–6 the Army of Northern Virginia waded across the wide but shallow Potomac River near Leesburg and entered Maryland. It bore no resemblance to what one imagines a conquering army to be. Uniforms were rags, faces were unshaven, unkempt hair was sticking out of torn hats. The barefooted seemed to outnumber those with shoes. A young civilian watching the columns pass stated: "They were the dirtiest men I ever saw, a most ragged, lean, and hungry set of wolves." Another witness confessed that she felt a certain sympathy for "this horde of ragamuffins" because "some were limping along so painfully, trying to keep up with their comrades."[3]

Lee advanced to Frederick, the principal town in the western part of Maryland. As Confederates

rested, the commander took an up-to-date look at the military situation. Three things gave him concern: The people of Maryland had not greeted his soldiers warmly; McClellan's Army of the Potomac was giving chase sooner than expected; and a 12,000-man Union garrison at Harpers Ferry to Lee's rear was still there. Harpers Ferry lay astride Lee's main lines of transportation and communication. Those 12,000 Federals were large enough to be a serious threat.

Under the circumstances, the Confederate army could not continue its northward march toward the second most important city in the Union: Harrisburg, Pennsylvania. Lee determined instead to pursue again the dangerous tactic of splitting his small army. This time he would do so in enemy territory, and he would divide his force into several pieces.

Longstreet was to march twenty-seven miles west across South Mountain toward Hagerstown in the valley beyond. General D. Harvey Hill's division would be posted at the passes atop South Mountain to slow down any Union pursuit. Meanwhile, Jackson would march back to Harpers Ferry and approach the garrison from three different directions. Once Jackson had secured Harpers Ferry, he would join Lee and Longstreet in the Maryland extension of the Shenandoah Valley.

The great French general Napoleon Bonaparte always felt that an army should be scattered while marching and concentrated when fighting. Lee was taking the first part of that principle to an extreme. To make sure that his instructions

Above: Ragged Confederate
soldiers removed or rolled up
their trousers as Lee's army
waded across the Potomac River
into Maryland.

were clear, Lee spelled out the army's several movements in Special Orders No. 191. Copies went to each corps and division commander.

On September 10 the six parts of Lee's army left Frederick in four directions.[4] Confederate campfires were still warm when McClellan's huge force began filing slowly into town. Then the greatest security leak in American military history occurred. A Union soldier found three cigars wrapped in a paper on which there was a good deal of writing. Soon McClellan was looking at a copy of Special Orders No. 191, Army of Northern Virginia.

The Union general knew not only that Lee's little army was in several scattered pieces; he knew where the pieces were and how long they intended to be there! McClellan was as familiar with Confederate plans as if he had been in Lee's tent when the movements were discussed. Small wonder that McClellan exclaimed: "Here is a piece of paper with which if I cannot whip Bobbie Lee, I will be willing to go home."[5]

Over 90,000 Federal soldiers started west toward South Mountain and Lee's 40,000 scattered men. It took all-day fighting on September 14 for McClellan to gain control of the mountain passes. He was now closer to Lee, and closer to Jackson, than the two Confederate generals were to each other. Lee was preparing to order a general withdrawal when word came from Jackson: the Harpers Ferry garrison would be seized the next day. Lee knew of McClellan's slowness. The Southern general determined to wait and see what Jackson would do.

Opposite: **Commanding half of Lee's army on the first Northern invasion was General James Longstreet (1821-1904). This South Carolina native was large in size and strong in opinion. Unbreakable on defense, Longstreet left something to be desired on offense.**

Early on the morning of the fifteenth Jackson unleashed a tremendous artillery bombardment on Harpers Ferry. The gunfire was so heavy and so accurate that the 12,000 Federals inside the town surrendered before 8:00 a.m.[6] Jackson left General A. P. Hill's division to secure the post and take care of prisoners. He then led the remainder of his command on a hard, rapid march north to reunite with Lee.

McClellan, perched atop South Mountain, spent the day watching the two wings of the enemy come back together. Had the Union forces moved speedily, they could have driven between Lee and Jackson and soundly defeated each segment in turn. However, swift movements were never part of McClellan's generalship. Nor was battle. He was too proud of his army to expose it to bloody action. "I am to watch over you as a parent over his children," he once announced to his soldiers, "and you know that your General loves you from the depths of his heart."[7]

The old doubts and feelings of uncertainty now overcame McClellan again. Fearing defeat more than wanting victory, he watched and waited for some opportunity to do something.

For Lee, it was one thing to abandon the march toward Pennsylvania; it was another to return to Virginia without a fight. Lee knew that McClellan would have to attack sooner or later. The Union general could not ignore the Confederate army on Northern soil. As long as it was there, Lee was winning the campaign.

On September 16, Lee moved to Sharpsburg to hasten the reunion with Jackson's columns. Barely 1,300 people lived in Sharpsburg. Most of them were German Baptist Brethren, or "Dunkers," who had never wanted anything but to live in peace. Lee pointed to the high ground north and east of the village. "We will make a stand on those hills," he said.[8]

Confederates formed battle lines on the semicircular ridge that curved from the Potomac River through farmland and ended at Antietam Creek. The stream was wide enough and deep enough to require bridges for an army to cross. Only one bridge of note was in the area where Lee proposed to do battle. His battle line was short, only four miles in length. There were places from which he could see the entire field of combat. Lee's preparations reflected his skill as an army engineer.

Despite the strength of his position, Lee was in some danger at Sharpsburg. His army was still miles inside enemy country. Only two narrow roads offered an escape route to the south. The Potomac River was three miles behind Lee. If his line should break under attack, at least part of it could be driven into a river uncrossable except at certain points. Desperate fighting,

solid teamwork, and outstanding leadership would all have to be in place if the Confederates were to withstand an attack from a force two and one half times the size of their own.

By the predawn hours of Wednesday, September 17, McClellan had his army in position. An attack in force at every point would almost certainly have broken Lee's lines in one or more places. Instead, the cautious McClellan decided to make his assaults in stages by hitting one sector of Lee's line at a time.

The first wave of Federals struck Jackson's soldiers on the Confederate left around 6:00 a.m. Some of the most intense combat of the war took place in a cornfield and two stands of woods bordered by split-rail fences. Every green stalk in the field was shredded by gunfire. Hand-to-hand fighting occurred amid thick gray smoke. The roar of musketry became mixed with the screams of wounded and dying soldiers. Acres of ground became covered with bodies.

Jackson's line bent, and bent some more, but it never broke. For the third time in the Civil War (after First and Second Manassas), Jackson earned the nickname "Stonewall." Two full Union corps could not pierce Jackson's position, although 5,500 soldiers fell dead or wounded fighting for control of the grounds around a Dunker church. At 9:00 a.m. the Union attacks against Lee's left weakened and then stopped.

Throughout the action, Lee shifted men from other parts of his defensive line to Jackson's threatened position. This process is called "inner lines of defense." No general in

the Civil War did it better than Lee.

McClellan's first effort had been bloodily repulsed. The Union commander then turned his attention to the Confederate center. Southern troops were massed on a country road that ran along the bottom of some high ground. Years of use had caused the road to become sunken. Confederates piled boards, stones, and other cover in front of it to make the road one of the strongest defenses in the war.

At midmorning fresh lines of Federals moved down the hill toward the sunken road. Confederate musketry ripped through the columns. Federals regrouped and tried again. Southerners inflicted more punishment. From the hillside to the road, a distance of

Above: **Stonewall Jackson's men caught the first fury of the Union's assaults on Antietam.**

Above: **Shown here are the mess kit and field glasses used by Lee throughout the war.**

only a few yards, the two sides exchanged volleys for an hour or more. Heavy numbers of Federals and dwindling ammunition among the Confederates led to the abandonment of the road. Lee ordered the survivors to take a new position farther back. The Army of Northern Virginia was battered and bloody, but it was still intact and in place.

At this time the one cannon left in the four-gun Rockbridge Artillery passed Lee. Among the dirty, exhausted cannoneers was Robert E. Lee Jr. "General," the lad called out to his father, "are you going to send us in again?"

"Yes, my son," Lee answered, "you must all do

what you can to help drive those people back."[9]

Vicious fighting was taking its toll on the Confederates. Lee's position was becoming more desperate by the hour. His ranks were getting thinner, good officers were falling every minute, and Lee was reaching a point where he had no troops to send to points in danger. Making everything worse was the pain shooting up his arms from the injured hands.

The third stage of the battle came in the afternoon. General Ambrose Burnside's Union corps fought its way across the one bridge in the area spanning Antietam Creek. It struck the undermanned Southern line that was Lee's right flank. Confederates gave way. They retreated slowly, making the Federals pay dearly for every foot of ground. Lee's line was bending back and away from the roads leading to Virginia. The Army of Northern Virginia was slowly being encircled.

Suddenly, through the dust and low-hanging battle smoke, Lee saw a line of soldiers coming from the south. He feared it might be a Union force moving in for the kill. The red, low-slanting sun then revealed that it was General A. P. Hill's large Confederate division arriving from Harpers Ferry after a seventeen-mile forced march. Hill's men slammed into the side of Burnside's advancing ranks. A heated fight continued for several minutes. Federals broke under the flank assault and dashed for safety back across the creek. The sun then set, and the great Battle of Antietam ended for all except the wounded. Their

moans and cries would fill the nighttime hours.

By then a Boston newspaper correspondent said in a dispatch, "All the country was flaming, smoking, and burning, as if the last great day, the Day of Judgment of the Lord, had come."[10]

It had been a day of bloodletting unequaled in all of our nation's history. Over 23,000 men had been killed, injured, or captured. The casualties at Antietam were more than the Americans lost in the Revolutionary War, the War of 1812, and the Mexican War *combined*.

It was victory and a defeat for both sides. Lee had pulled the Union army from Virginia; he had captured 12,000 soldiers at Harpers Ferry; his men had hurled back every major attack made against them along Antietam Creek. Until this engagement Lee had allowed his subordinate officers to conduct movements on their own. At Antietam, Lee himself shifted his undermanned forces here and there to meet heavy Union attacks made over a twelve-hour period. Lee was not pleased at the outcome of the battle, but in time he became more proud of Antietam than any other engagement he directed because he felt his men had faced the heaviest odds they had ever encountered.[11]

If Lee's fighting spirits were high, so was his temper. During the battle he saw one of Stonewall Jackson's soldiers heading for the rear with a squealing pig. Lee angrily ordered the man seized and taken to Jackson for immediate execution. Jackson was too hard-pressed for troops to waste a life. He put the infantryman back in the ranks. The man performed bravely, which prompted one of Lee's staff officers to remark that the skulker had "lost his pig but saved his bacon."[12]

Lee stood defiantly in battle position the next day. The Union army did not resume its assaults. Lee used the cover of night to withdraw from Sharpsburg and start back to Virginia. None of his hopes for the Northern invasion had been realized.

Never did McClellan have a more splendid occasion to destroy the Army of Northern Virginia. Yet he repeatedly fumbled away his opportunities. Not once did the Union army assail Lee's lines with full strength. McClellan kept much of his force in reserve in case he was defeated on the field. Even with the Confederate army in full retreat, the Union commander made only a small, halfhearted attempt to stop Lee.

In the end, nevertheless, the greater successes went to the North. The Army of the Potomac had stopped a Confederate invasion. Lee's efforts to gain favor in Maryland came to naught. So did hopes of any European recognition and aid. Antietam might have been a military disappointment in the eyes of the Union government, but it was a decisive political triumph.

President Lincoln saw enough good in Antietam to feel justified in issuing a preliminary

Right: Antietam produced scores of scenes like this. Destruction, wounds, and death marked every sector of the battle.

Emancipation Proclamation. For the Union, the Civil War thereafter became a struggle with twin goals: to restore the Union and to end slavery in America. A new and more intense conflict now began. This is why many historians view Antietam as the high point in the life of the Confederate States.

England and France both backed farther away from the Southern cause rather than be labeled defenders of slavery. Henry Adams, American ambassador to England, wrote from London that "the Emancipation Proclamation has done more for us here than all our former victories and all our diplomacy."[13]

Once Lee's forces reached the safety of the Shenandoah Valley, the general began to restore, resupply, and drill his army. His hands continued to heal slowly. Lee recommended that both Longstreet and Jackson be promoted to lieutenant general and given command of the two corps in the army. Stragglers returned to duty. New recruits entered camp in a steady stream. Soon the Southern army was back to its strength when Lee took command in front of Richmond. The ranks were in good fighting trim.

Lee's organizational skills after three months in army command were outstanding. He had turned his divisions into a fighting machine that had absolute confidence in itself and him. Morale is always the basic test of an army. Morale under Lee was high in every regiment. His soldiers came to say of Lee: "He looks after his men."[14] That simple statement explains what a real leader should be.

The general had become a man who scorned informality and encouraged respect. While subordinates called one another by last name, Lee was always "the general."[15] He himself addressed officers by their rank. One reason for this was that Lee was twenty years older than most of them.

Lee commanded respect by his very presence. An English reporter visiting the Confederate encampments in mid-October 1862 described Lee as "the incarnation of health and endurance . . . his manner calm and stately, his presence impressive and imposing, his dark brown eyes remarkably direct and honest as they meet you fully and firmly." Lee was so courteous and gentle, the newspaperman added, that "a child thrown among a knot of strangers would inevitably be drawn to him . . . and would run to claim his protection."[16]

The general always shied away from praise. He wrote his wife at this time: "I tremble for my country when I hear of confidence expressed in me. I know too well my weakness, and that our only hope is in God."[17]

Lee expected no interference from McClellan in the post-Antietam weeks, and none came. The bloodshed in Maryland had so shocked the Union general that he made no move against Lee for over a month. One of the excuses he gave Lincoln for his inactivity was the weariness of the army horses. The president replied sarcastically: "Will you pardon me for asking what the horses of your army have done since the battle of Antietam that would fatigue anything?"[18]

Robert E. Lee

Left: Ambrose E. Burnside (1824-1881) was a jovial and likeable officer. Unfortunately, he lacked the vision and drive to be a successful army commander.

Above: Pictured here are two of the Union pontoon bridges spanning the Rappahannock River in Fredericksburg, Virginia. Union soldiers marched across them to attack the Confederates posted on high ground in the distance.

Robert E. Lee

Late in October, McClellan eased his large army into Virginia. Lee was then in the midst of trying to recover from the sudden death of his second daughter. Twenty-three-year-old Annie Lee had contracted typhoid fever. It quickly proved fatal. The general's grief would be profound for the next month.

He reacted to McClellan's move by again splitting his forces. Jackson's half remained in Shenandoah Valley near Winchester. Longstreet's corps crossed the Blue Ridge Mountains and took a position in the northern piedmont around Culpeper. This division would enable one wing of Lee's army to strike if McClellan applied pressure to the other wing.

Such did not take place because Lincoln's patience with McClellan became exhausted. Early in November, after elections in the North insured a Republican majority in the Congress, Lincoln removed McClellan from command. Lee read the news with some regret. He said of McClellan: "We always understood each other so well. I fear they may continue to make these changes till they find someone whom I don't understand."[19]

Lee had little difficulty in understanding General Ambrose Burnside. This Rhode Islander who succeeded McClellan at the head of the Union army was a hearty, well-liked officer but woefully lacking in military judgment. Burnside knew that he had been appointed to fight. He quickly shifted his army toward Fredericksburg. The plan was to cross the Rappahannock River there, get behind Lee's divided command, and drive straight for Richmond.

The Union hope for a secret and speedy movement collapsed. Burnside and his army of 120,000 soldiers had to wait a month for pontoons to arrive before crossing the Rappahannock. By the time they were in place, Lee and all of his army—78,000 men—were on high ground behind Fredericksburg. Lee had developed one of the strongest defensive positions in nineteenth-century warfare.

Burnside should have made new plans. Instead, he displayed no imagination from start to end. Union artillery opened a point-blank fire into the buildings of Fredericksburg. Civilians as well as soldiers huddled helplessly inside the structures. Such cruelty sparked anger in Lee. "Those people," he said with emotion, "delight to destroy the weak and those who can make no defense. It just suits them!"[20]

What occurred on December 13 was not a battle, but a slaughter. Burnside hurled division after division across open ground into the face of rifle and artillery fire from a strong and confident opponent. Lee's lines were simply unbreakable. Thirteen times the Union army attacked; thirteen times it fell back in bloody repulse. Early in the battle Lee had some concern over the thousands of Union soldiers surging toward his lines. He voiced his feeling to Longstreet, who replied bluntly: "General, if you put every man on the other side of the Potomac in that field to approach me over the same line, and give me plenty of ammunition,

I will kill them all before they reach my line!"[21]

Dead and dying Union soldiers literally covered the mile-wide expanse of land between Lee's earthworks and the town. From mid morning until sundown, not one Union soldier got to within 100 yards of Lee's position at Marye's Heights. In the space of an acre or so lay 1,100 dead Federals, some of them piled eight deep.[22]

For Lee, Fredericksburg was markedly different from Antietam. In western Maryland there had been great tension and uneasiness as the powerful Union army crashed into Lee from three different directions. Lee had to move troops desperately from here to there to avoid defeat. At Fredericksburg, Lee watched the Army of the Potomac self-destruct against strongly entrenched Confederates. At one point in the contest a grim Lee turned to Longstreet and remarked: "It is well that war is so terrible; else we should grow too fond of it."[23]

Other soldiers also felt a sense of pity in the one-sided contest. Richard Kirkland was a nineteen-year-old sergeant from South Carolina. He became highly distressed over the cries of "water, water" from wounded enemy soldiers lying in front of his position. Kirkland obtained permission to climb out of the trench. For the better part of two hours he carried canteens of water to every badly injured Federal he could reach. Not one shot was fired at the young Confederate throughout that period. Kirkland became known on both sides thereafter as the "Angel of Marye's Heights."[24]

The night of December 13 was black only for

a few minutes. Then a ghostly light began on the horizon and grew in brightness until it made a wide arc across the sky. Shafts of color seemed to stand still. So did Confederate and Union soldiers paralyzed by the unusual aurora borealis ("northern lights") that few of them had ever seen. The sight excited one Confederate private. "We enthusiastic young fellows felt that the heavens were hanging out banners and streamers and setting off fireworks in honor of our victory."[25]

Burnside lost more than 12,600 men at Fredericksburg. The Union army limped back across the Rappahannock River. Lee did not pursue. His position was ideal as a defense, but his army could not launch a counterattack against superior numbers. Fredericksburg was another "empty victory" for Lee. As he wrote the secretary of war a month later: "The lives of our soldiers are too precious to be sacrificed in the attainment of successes that inflict no loss upon the enemy beyond the actual loss in battle. Every victory should bring us nearer to the great end which it is the object of this war to reach."[26]

Phillips

Lacy

Burnside

Canal

Fredericksburg

Fredericksburg

Plank Road

Marye

Hazel Run

Longstreet

unfinished railroad

Lee Hill

Telegraph Road

Lee

Richmond, Fredericksburg & Potomac

Stafford Heights

Riverside Road

Mansfield

Deep Run

Rappahannock River

Smithfield

Bernard's Cabins

Meade

Military Road

Prospect Hill

River Road

Mine Road

Jackson

Hamilton's Crossing

Hamilton

0   1
Miles

Loss of an Arm

The year 1863 had just begun when a Wisconsin soldier wrote home from a snowy camp near Fredericksburg. Across the Rappahannock River, he stated, was "a skillfully posted, victorious army, under the eye of a vigilant and war-wise general, always ready and determined to resist the passage of any Union force."[1]

Victorious and vigilant the Confederate army was, but it was also hungry and ill-equipped. Lee's headquarters tent was in thick pinewoods on the railroad below Fredericksburg. He lived simply. Knowing that his food was no better than that of his men, Lee could joke about it. An aide observed that the hard biscuits were indigestible. Lee replied: "They will stick with you longer."[2]

Soldiers lived in little wooden huts they built from nearby timber. A few of the men preferred tents, to which chimneys made of barrels were attached. The need for building materials and firewood caused the cutting down of hundreds of trees. As a result, the army camp stood in a large open space that offered no shade or cover.

Lee's men looked more like scarecrows than soldiers. Uniforms were in rags. A large number were without shoes. Worst of all, they were hungry. Their daily rations were a few ounces of cornmeal and bacon, with whatever sassafras roots and onions they could find growing wild. Sometimes the bacon was so spoiled that it smelled too foul to eat. Heavy rains and snow added to the misery. "We are in a liquid state at present," Lee wrote home. "Up to our knees in mud."[3]

Most of the animals had been sent elsewhere to obtain forage. Many horses and mules had to be kept near the front. They were thin and always hungry—so hungry that they often gnawed at the bark of trees still standing. Every tree was stripped of bark as high as horses could use their teeth.

Lee had a great love of animals. He grieved at the suffering of the horses, as well as at the hunger of his soldiers. Much of the burden of the army he bore on his shoulders as if he were responsible for all of the needs of his men. "His theory, expressed on many occasions," wrote a staff officer, "was that the private soldiers . . . were the most meritorious class

Above: Religion was the greatest
source of morale in Civil War
armies. Lee often joined his men
in prayer around a campfire.

of the army, and that they deserved and should receive the utmost respect and consideration."[4]

The soldiers knew Lee's feelings, and they returned the affection wholeheartedly. A surgeon told his wife: "It does not seem possible to defeat this army now with General Lee at its head."[5] A Virginia private later recalled: "It was remarkable what confidence the men reposed in General Lee; they were ready to follow him wherever he might lead, or order them to go."[6]

Such love for their commander did not prevent homesickness from being ever present in the ranks. One day that winter Union and Confederate bands began playing on opposite banks of the Rappahannock. Each time a band played "Dixie" or "The Battle Hymn of the Republic," men on both sides cheered.

Then, near sundown, a lone bugler began the notes of the all-time favorite song of the war, "Home, Sweet Home." Some 150,000 Johnny Rebs and Billy Yanks together tried to sing the melody. Most could not. A Union soldier explained: "As the sweet sounds rose and fell on the evening air, all listened intently, and I don't believe there was a dry eye in all those assembled thousands." The song ended. Soldiers silently stared into the darkness, each man wrapped in thoughts of loved ones at home.[7]

Living in the face of death, many soldiers found comfort and strength in religion. The winter of 1862–63 brought the first of several "Great Revivals" sweeping through Lee's army. Missionaries and visiting ministers joined army chaplains in the field. Prayer meetings,

baptisms, and Bible studies occurred several days a week. Lee and the pious Jackson greatly encouraged such religious ceremonies. On one occasion the two generals sat together on a log at a field service. Both men wept at a sermon that spoke of home and loved ones far away.[8]

Suddenly, on March 30, 1863, Lee fell gravely ill for the first time in his life. It began with a sore throat, but other symptoms—fever, elevated pulse, pain in the chest and arms—suggest strongly that Lee may have had some form of heart attack. For two weeks he was unable to function normally. Lee complained privately that the physicians "were tapping me all over like an old steam boiler before condemning it."[9]

In public Lee displayed high spirits. One physician noted that the general was "always polite and agreeable, and thinking less of himself than he aught to . . . hoping and praying for nothing but the success of our cause and the return of blessed peace."[10]

He returned to duty in mid-April, much to the joy of the army. "Genl. Lee is getting better so I am informed much to my pleasure," one of his brigadiers wrote. "It would be a real misfortune for him to be away from us at this time."[11]

Opposite: The third commander of the Army of the Potomac was Joseph Hooker (1814-1879). Handsome and boastful, Hooker would break under pressure once Lee seized the offensive.

Loss of an Arm

Above: Chancellorsville, Virginia, was nothing more than the imposing Chancellor mansion set at a vital crossroads in the Wilderness. There, Hooker made his headquarters and concentrated his army.

Robert E. Lee

That officer was correct. The Union army across the river was stirring for a new campaign. General Joseph Hooker had taken command of the Army of the Potomac. A skilled organizer and motivator, Hooker rebuilt the army to more than twice Lee's strength. In the process of reorganization Hooker gave the soldiers a new belief in themselves. He had earned the nickname "Fighting Joe" because he was aggressive and confident. Hooker's battle plan for that spring seemed on paper to be unbeatable.

He would leave 40,000 troops at Fredericksburg to occupy Lee's attention. A heavy Union cavalry raid behind Lee's lines would cut communications between the Southern army and Richmond. Meanwhile, Hooker, with 70,000 soldiers, would move secretly up the Rappahannock, cross it and the Rapidan River, and get on Lee's left flank. If Lee remained where he was, he would be caught between two huge Union forces. If Lee fell back, Hooker would strike his flank on ground of Hooker's own choosing.

General Porter Alexander of the Confederacy thought the plan "the best strategy conceived by the enemy against the Army of Northern Virginia" in the war.[12] Hooker thought so too. He told his officers: "My plans are perfect, and when I start to carry them out, may God have mercy on General Lee, for I will have none."[13]

In the final days of April the Union movement began. It was quite similar to Lee's strategy at Second Manassas in sending Jackson around Pope's flank. Long columns of Federals marched twenty miles to the west, crossed the Rappahannock and the Rapidan, and turned east into a heavily wooded region known as "the Wilderness." As soon as Hooker's lead units emerged from that dark and gloomy woodland, they would be on Lee's exposed flank. That would turn Lee out of his strong position at Fredericksburg and force him into battle in the open.

Lee seemed in a doomed position. Yet from the start, Hooker had made a fatal error: He assumed that Lee would react as Hooker expected him to do. Lee was never predictable. Nor was he a commander who would sit and wait to be destroyed.

Because he was so heavily outnumbered and pinned between two large Union forces, Lee could take enormous risks. He did so by launching an offensive of his own—a countermeasure even bolder than Hooker's movements. It began, as Lee's strategy had so often done, with a splitting of his forces in the face of superior numbers of the enemy.

One Confederate division would remain in front of General John Sedgwick's Union host at Fredericksburg. Lee would take his remaining 42,000 troops west to confront Hooker somewhere near the Wilderness. Jackson's men took the lead. Federals were just emerging from the Wilderness when, on May 1, Jackson struck with his usual fury.

The action stunned Hooker. Because his cavalry was on a raid, the Union general was blind to Confederate movements. Jackson's sudden attack shattered Hooker's thinking that Lee would have no choice but to flee or be defeated. The Union commander now lost all enthusiasm. He recalled his army back into the Wilderness. Orders went forth for the Federals to prepare a defensive position.

Earthworks and log fortifications quickly took shape in the dense forest. Hooker was headquartered in a brick home on the left of the line just inside the Wilderness. The lone residence stood at the junction of two country roads known by the name of Chancellorsville.

Lee could not understand why Hooker was retreating into an area where he could not maneuver. Nor would Federal superiority in artillery be of any use to him in the trees and underbrush. In short, Hooker had given up the offensive. Lee moved quickly to take it.

On the night of May 1, Lee and Jackson conferred while seated in the woods on cracker boxes. It seemed almost impossible to find a way to drive Hooker's 70,000 Federals through the Wilderness and over the Rappahannock. Then cavalry chief Jeb Stuart galloped to a stop with amazing news: The Union right flank was "in the air." It was neither anchored on a strong point nor bent back for protection. The Union right simply extended three miles west of Chancellorsville and stopped.

By the light of a few lanterns, Lee and Jackson then "designed one of the boldest tactical actions in modern warfare."[14] Jackson would make a secret, wide-circling march of twelve miles to get on the exposed enemy flank. Once that was accomplished, he would unleash a surprise attack and roll up the Union line from west to east.

Lee asked how many men Jackson intended to take. My whole corps, came the response. Lee was surprised that 28,000 men would make the march. That left only 14,000 soldiers for Lee to face Hooker's entire force of five times that number. Should Hooker realize Lee's predicament and attack, the Confederate army would be destroyed and Richmond left helpless. Lee thought only for a moment. The stakes were high, but victory would be sweet. He turned to Jackson. "Well, go on."[15]

Jackson began the flank movement shortly after dawn on May 2. Had his men been able to average their usual two miles per hour, they would have been in attack position near noon. Yet for most of the long march the men were using abandoned wagon trails where there were roads at all. The column strung out and began to lose distance. Jackson galloped back and forth along the lines. "Keep the columns closed!" he urged. "Press on, press on!"[16]

Soon Jackson's corps stretched for six miles. It was tough going, but far in the rear men could be heard exclaiming: "Tell Old Jack we're all a-coming! . . . Don't let him begin the fun till we git thar!"[17]

At 5:15 p.m. Jackson had two of his three divisions in position. Only three hours of daylight remained. Jackson gave the signal. A

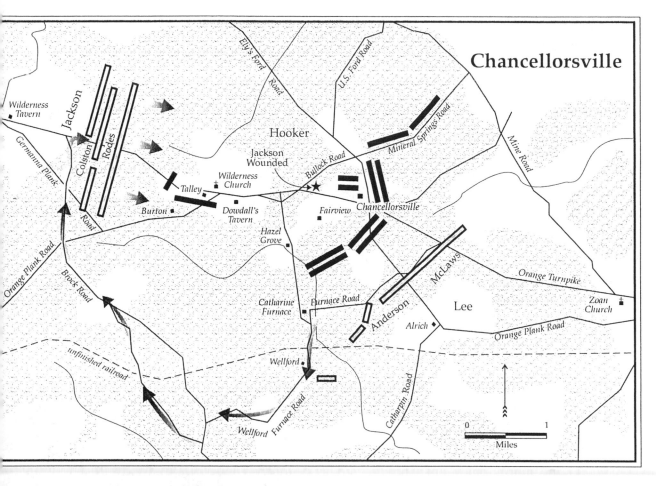

Chancellorsville

Wilderness
Tavern

Jackson

Ely's Ford Road

U.S. Ford Road

Hooker

Colston

Rodes

Jackson
Wounded

Germanna Plank

Talley

Wilderness
Church

Bullock Road

Mineral Springs Road

Mine Road

Burton

Orange Plank Road

Road

Dowdall's
Tavern

Fairview

Chancellorsville

Hazel
Grove

Brock Road

Catharine
Furnace

Furnace Road

McLaws

Orange Turnpike

Zoan
Church

unfinished railroad

Wellford

Anderson

Lee

Alrich

Orange Plank Road

Catharpin Road

Wellford Furnace Road

0   1

Miles

Above: **Stonewall Jackson's most famous flank march was a twelve-mile movement that put his twenty-eight thousand soldiers on the unprotected end of the Union army. The resultant attack came too late in the day to achieve total victory.**

Confederate battle line two miles wide began advancing through the woods.

Union soldiers were lounging in camp. Their rifles were stacked. Those not writing letters or napping were fixing supper. Suddenly, rabbits and other creatures came bounding through the brush. Then Confederates crashed through the thickets. As the attacks gained momentum Jackson's men broke into the spine-chilling "rebel yell."

The sheer force of the attack overwhelmed an entire Union corps. A Pennsylvania officer confessed: "The Plank road, and woods that bordered it, presented a scene of terror and confusion. Men and animals were dashing against one another in wild dismay before the line of fire that came cracking and crashing after them."[18]

One reason Jackson was so successful was Robert E. Lee. The commander had spent all of May 2 having his small force make movements and noise visible enough and loud enough to hold Hooker's attention. Lee's anxiety grew as he watched the Federals and waited for Jackson's attack. When it came, Lee offered what support he could in the fading sunlight and gun smoke.

Darkness brought an end to the first day's fighting at Chancellorsville. Jackson had driven the Federals three miles. Hooker's line, originally a shallow curve along the Plank Road, now resembled a V. As the gunfire slackened with the coming of night, tragedy occurred for the Confederates. Jackson was

Above: **Union artilleries frantically tried to meet Jackson's assault, which stretched for two miles from end to end.**

Above: Virginia soldier and artist William L. Sheppard captured in one of his paintings a scene of Confederates overrunning the Union earthworks at Chancellorsville late in the afternoon.

accidentally shot by his own men.[19] Lee was deeply concerned at this news, but he could not let Jackson's wounds interfere with the course of the battle.

Fighting resumed with the dawn of May 3. Near noon Lee's forces and those of Jackson united and closed on the center of Hooker's line. Lee started forward to direct the pursuit. The Chancellor house was now in flames, as if it were a bonfire celebrating the victory. This was "the supreme moment of [Lee's] life as a soldier. The sun of his destiny was at its zenith."[20]

Captain Richard York of the 6th North Carolina later remembered: "Suddenly we saw passing through the thin woods on a little hill in our rear, Gen. Lee. As soon as his face was well seen, and known to be certainly he, every man instinctively commenced getting ready. The word soon went down the line 'All is right, Uncle Robert is here. We will whip them.' There was no cheering. The men leaned on their muskets and looked at him, as he rode along his lines, as tho' a God were passing by. No one thought of tossing his cap, or hurrahing. The safe, implicit confidence in security, the certainty of success, the lifting of the terrible doubt that hung over us, was more than cap-tossing or shouting."[21]

This great spectacle was short-lived. Two messages shattered the mood. Jackson's surgeon had been forced to amputate the general's shattered arm. Tearfully, Lee told a chaplain friend: "Give him my affectionate regards. . . .

He has lost his left arm but I have lost my right."[22]

A second dispatch informed Lee that Sedgwick's Union force had crossed the river at Fredericksburg, driven the thin line of Confederate defenders from the high ground, and was marching toward Chancellorsville to strike Lee. The commander detached a single division eastward to check this advance as long as possible. Lee waited a day. When Hooker showed no sign of resuming an offense, Lee hastened with half of his army to attack Sedgwick.

Sharp and bloody fighting at Salem Church first checked Sedgwick and then sent his troops in retreat across the Rappahannock. Lee then turned back toward Chancellorsville with the hope of delivering a deathblow to Hooker's wing of the Union army. Weary and battle-thinned Confederate ranks drew up in attack position on the night of May 5. Dawn found no enemy in sight. Hooker had given up the campaign and retired beyond the river.

Chancellorsville was Lee's most stunning victory. He had not only soundly defeated in open battle an enemy twice his size, he had also shattered the most concentrated Union strategy yet launched against his army. Hooker had suffered almost 17,000 casualties. Confederate losses were 13,100 men. When news of the success swept across the South, a Texas plantation girl spoke a nation's praise when she called the victor "Lee the invincible."[23]

Above: **This highly exaggerated drawing shows Lee advancing with his soldiers toward victory as the Chancellor mansion burns in the background. Lee would hardly have been the only mounted officer in the attack.**

All of the joy ended on May 10, when Lee received the message he had prayed would not come. Stonewall Jackson had died from his wounds.

The bond between Lee and Jackson had always been a curious one. Seventeen years apart in age, they had scarcely known each other until civil war and the defense of Virginia brought them together. Lee was dignified and diplomatic; Jackson was difficult to know and stern. They had deep but different religions. Jackson was an Old Testament warrior who believed in total destruction as waged by Joshua and David. Lee was more New Testament, a soldier who exhibited compassion even in combat.

Working together, the two men were almost a model military partnership. "So great is my confidence in General Lee," Jackson once declared, "that I am willing to follow him blindfolded." At Jackson's death a grief-stricken Lee admitted: "I know not how to replace him."[24]

Lee would find no replacement. Jackson had given Lee the one thing the smaller Army of Northern Virginia had to have to survive against larger Union forces. That ingredient was mobility. Jackson's presence had permitted Lee to divide his army and undertake bold flank marches. This kept the enemy off-balance and subject to surprise attacks. After Jackson's passing, Lee could not find a substitute capable of making those lightning strikes. After Chancellorsville, Lee would not attempt the spectacular splitting of his army that he had done not once, but five times with Jackson.

Now Jackson was gone. Lee and the Army of Northern Virginia would never again be what they had been.

Above: **The death of Stonewall Jackson was the greatest personal blow the South suffered during the war. Never again did the Army of Northern Virginia fight with the daring and aggressiveness it had shown when Jackson was present.**

Below: General Richard S. Ewell (1817-1872) replaced Jackson at the head of the Second Corps, but he lacked Stonewall's drive and determination.

Right: One of the finest division commanders in military history, A. Powell Hill (1825-1865) fell ill just after a promotion to corps command and had a spotty performance thereafter.

Robert E. Lee

Gettysburg

How to replace Jackson occupied Lee's thoughts in the days immediately after Chancellorsville. No choice was obvious. Lee therefore reorganized the two corps in the Army of Northern Virginia into three corps. Longstreet retained command of the First Corps, Richard S. Ewell took most of Jackson's soldiers for the Second Corps, and A. P. Hill was promoted to head of the new Third Corps.

Ewell seemed a good selection because he had been the most conspicuous of Jackson's division commanders in the 1862 valley campaign. He was a curious but generally likable man. Bulging eyes, a sweeping mustachio, a high-pitched voice that bellowed curses, and the movements of a startled bird made "Old Baldhead Ewell" a character in the army. At Second Manassas in August 1862 he had lost a leg. He just now had returned to duty, not well, but eager to get back in the field.

"Little Powell" Hill had won his promotion in battle. The slim, redheaded Virginian was an impetuous, hard-fighting general who had led the largest division in Lee's army. Hill was a no-nonsense officer, plainly dressed. A lieutenant once described him as having "an old white hat slouched down over his eyes, his coat off and wearing an old flannel shirt, looking as mean as a bull."[1]

While shuffling his army into a new alignment, Lee also had to resist losing part of it. The vital river port of Vicksburg, Mississippi, was then under siege. Confederate officials wanted to transfer troops from Lee's army to the West. Lee opposed such a move for understandable reasons. The Confederacy could afford to lose the West and still win the Civil War. Yet the Southern nation could not lose the East and triumph. The East was the main theater—the focal point of Northern as well as European attention. To take advantage of the situation in the East, Lee came forth with a plan to make a second invasion of the North.

His advance was to be the main effort in a large strategy on behalf of the whole Confederacy. A march into the North would enable Lee's army to feed on enemy supplies and at the same time pull the Union army from Virginia. This strike might force the Union to relieve the pressure on both Vicksburg and Chattanooga, Tennessee. If Lee was victorious, his presence in Pennsylvania would surely discourage the enemy from sending reinforcements to the West. Further, a defeated Union army in the East would be forced to retreat northward across the Susquehanna River. This would give the Confederates at least temporary control over western Maryland and western Pennsylvania.

Such a strategy would surely convince the Northern population that the Confederacy was unconquerable and that the Union ought to accept an end to the war. If Lee's forces could maintain their superiority a few months longer, the Northern people could reject Lincoln and his Republican Party in the 1864 elections and replace them with an administration willing to make peace.

A final factor existed strongly inside Lee's army. Second Manassas, Fredericksburg, and Chancellorsville had been stunning Confederate successes. By the spring of 1863, Lee had given his army the habit of victory. Sergeant Daniel Lyon attended a field church service in mid-May and watched Lee closely. "As I sat on the ground in the hot boiling sun . . . and saw the Old General devoutly engaging in the service of the hour," Lyon wrote his wife, "my admiration of our Grand Old Hero was greater (if possible) than ever." Lyon added: "Such is the unbounded confidence in our Chieftain that we all care very little [where we go], as when we are ordered by him, we know it is the best place to go to. Genl.

Lee I believe has more brains than all the balance of our big men put together."[2]

Short on shoes and clothing, the Southern troops were nevertheless tough as leather. A wonderful bonding had occurred over the past year between leader and soldiers. They thought that Lee could do no wrong. Lee returned the adoration. He believed the Army of Northern Virginia capable of accomplishing anything.[3] A feeling of invincibility coursed through the ranks.

Lee was still not fully recovered from the illness of late March. He was now beginning to feel the aging process. Weariness came easier. Yet those factors did not dampen his optimism about the new campaign.

It got under way early in June. Leaving A. P. Hill's corps to face the Union army at Fredericksburg, and having both the Blue Ridge Mountains and Stuart's cavalry screening his movements, Lee was a week into his march before the enemy was aware of it. By then the advance guard of the Confederate army was splashing across the Potomac River above Harpers Ferry while the rear guard lingered near Fredericksburg.

Lee's 75,000 troops were strung out more than 100 miles in the hot summer sun. Lincoln urged Hooker to attack with the Army of the Potomac at some point. Hooker was unable to take the initiative. The nightmare of Chancellorsville still haunted him. On June 28, Lincoln removed Hooker from command. In his place the president appointed General George G. Meade.

Left: General George G. Meade (1815-1872) took command of the Army of the Potomac only three days before the battle of Gettysburg exploded. Meade was a solid rather than a brilliant leader—and one of Lee's oldest friends.

Above: This photograph of a section of the Gettysburg battlefield shows the broken terrain, hills, and fences that provided good defense and hindered Lee's attacks.

A professional soldier and an old friend of Lee's, Meade looked more like a clergyman than a general. That appearance concealed a proven field commander. Lee reacted to the news of a change of commanders by stating: "General Meade will make no blunder on my front, and if I make one he will make haste to take advantage of it."[4]

By late June all of Lee's army was in Pennsylvania and connected to its Virginia bases by the thinnest of threads. Confederates were on their own in a strange land. Lacking a

confused. No word had come from the cavalry-man since Lee entered Pennsylvania.

Lee was at Chambersburg when alarming news came: Meade had been in command for only two days, but he and the Union army were only thirty-five miles away. Lee quickly issued orders for his army—strung out over a vast area—to concentrate at Chambersburg. The Confederate invasion was over for the moment.

This gathering of Lee's army was still taking place when word came of a supply of shoes stored in nearby Gettysburg. Had Stuart's cavalry been at hand, the horsemen could have secured the needed shoes and perhaps learned more about the Union army's location. However, Stuart was nowhere in sight. A. P. Hill therefore dispatched a couple of infantry divisions to get the shoes. Gettysburg was only a village, yet it was the hub of a large number of roads. It could be the starting point for a movement in almost any direction.

Early on the morning of July 1, Hill's men reached Gettysburg and bumped into the lead elements of the enemy army. Heavy fighting began. Lee did not want to do battle at that time and place. He preferred to choose when and where the showdown with Meade's forces would be. Throughout the morning, Confederates got the better of it in the fighting. Lee soon arrived on the scene. The commander became convinced that his army was concentrating faster than Meade's forces. Lee made the fateful decision to press the enemy without delay.

The Gettysburg battlefield south of town

supply line, the army had to keep moving continually. If it did not, it would starve. Another dangerous element was present. Whenever and wherever Lee encountered the enemy, he had to strike without delay. The Army of Northern Virginia was an invading force and could not ignore a pursuing foe.

Worst of all, Lee was making his way through Pennsylvania "without eyes." Stuart's cavalry had been sent to collect supplies and information on the Federals. Lee had given Stuart wide latitude to keep any Union forces resembled an inverted question mark. At the northern tip of the question mark was Culp's Hill. High ground known as Cemetery Ridge then curved southward to a small prominence called Little Round Top. The dot of the question mark was Big Round Top. It was too detached and too steep to be of any importance in the battle. The entire Union line stretched four miles.

Throughout July 1, Confederates from west and north slowly drove two Union corps through Gettysburg and to the high ground beyond. The Union ranks were broken. A full attack by Lee would capture the elevated position. A. P. Hill's corps was too weak from the day's action to push farther. Lee then suggested to Ewell that his Second Corps make the assault. Ewell was not up to the task. He was a man accustomed to direct orders. When told to use his own judgment in his first fight since losing a leg, Ewell gave way to indecision and did nothing.

In spite of this failure, Lee had clearly won the first day's battle. Federals had been outnumbered and beaten. Lee's men had taken close to 5,000 prisoners. However, a number of things combined to work against the Southern commander.

First was the Union army. The ranks atop Cemetery Ridge were determined to hold fast for as long as it took the rest of the army to get to the field. A strange elevation of spirit had developed inside the hard-luck Army of the Potomac. "A feeling had taken hold of the army that it had suffered disasters enough," an Ohio soldier declared, "and that [its] time had now

come, whatever leader and at whatever cost."[5]

Lee still knew little about the enemy's whereabouts and had no cavalry to discover them. Two of his three corps commanders were still new to their jobs, while the third (Longstreet) had no confidence in Lee's plans. The Union army was moving into a defensive position. Lee could not prepare earthworks and fight back assaults as he had done at Antietam and Fredericksburg. It was too dangerous to try dazzling feints and flank marches deep in enemy territory. Meade would not be forced into Lee's kind of battle. Two armies were locked together. A slugging match had to follow.

This was the kind of fight that Lee had hoped to avoid from the beginning. Along with all of the elements working against him, Lee also had to battle health problems. His heart condition may not have become active again, but the general had fallen ill from chronic diarrhea. A Prussian officer who had ridden with the Confederate army for several months saw a change in Lee at Gettysburg. "The quiet, self-possessed calmness" was gone. "Lee was not at his ease, but was riding to and fro . . . making anxious inquiries here and there, and looking careworn."[6]

Sweeping victory on the first day had also made Lee overconfident. Thereafter came two days of poorly coordinated attacks against the best defensive position Lee's army had faced since Malvern Hill exactly a year ago.

A full moon that night lit the awful debris on the fields and hills where men had fought the

first day. July 2 came in hot. Lee was still with-
out precise information that his cavalry might
have provided. His battle plan was to attack the
Union left flank near the area of Little Round
Top. If successful, the assaults would cut the
Army of the Potomac's links to Washington and
Baltimore. Longstreet's corps would make the
great effort.

Longstreet was not in favor of launching an
offensive. His chief of staff admitted later that
the general "failed to conceal some anger" that
his opinions were not followed. "There was
apparent apathy in [Longstreet's] movements."[7]

The early-morning attacks that Lee wanted
did not begin until afternoon. What followed
were many separate fights, each one an hour or
so of concentrated fury. Confederates pounded

Above: Artist John Gilmer's
depiction of Lee riding among
the survivors returning from
the Pickett-Pettigrew Charge
on the third day of fighting.

Above: **Three Confederates taken prisoner at Gettysburg show the wide variety of "uniforms" worn by Lee's men midway during the war.**

the Union left head-on in a peach orchard, in a wheat field, and in a craggy ravine of large rocks known as Devil's Den. The whole area turned hot from desperate fighting. Above all the battle racket was the sound of cheering and cursing, while the fearful screams of dying men and horses gave a terrible overtone. Lines of infantry swayed in and out of the thick, drifting gun smoke. Battle flags were occasionally visible.

Killing continued until nightfall. Every Confederate assault that day had failed. Thousands of dead and injured soldiers lay in the fields and woods and rocky knolls separating the two armies.

To an ill Lee, disappointment was intense.

In midafternoon Stuart and his horsemen had rejoined the army. According to legend, Lee greeted his cavalry chief with a cold stare and said only: "Well, General Stuart, you are here at last."[8]

For July 3, Lee had two choices. He could acknowledge defeat and withdraw from the field, or he could attack again. Lee still considered his army unbeatable. One more concentrated attack, this time against the Union center, would bring the desired victory. Everything would come down to this final charge.

Both sides knew it. The two armies waited, tense, while the morning sun beat down on the battlefield. Lee called forward the fresh division of General George Pickett and added to it some troops from the divisions of Johnston Pettigrew and Isaac Trimble. At 1:00 p.m., 220 Confederate artillery opened fire to weaken the enemy position. Some 172 Federal guns a mile away answered, and for an hour the heaviest artillery exchange of the Civil War occurred.

One by one the Union guns began to grow silent. Confederates were convinced that the pieces had been disabled. In truth, Federals were withholding fire for the expected infantry assault. It came shortly after 3:00 p.m., when roughly 10,500 Southerners in parade fashion started across three quarters of a mile of open ground toward Cemetery Ridge and the Union lines.

The Pickett-Pettigrew charge was doomed from the start. Federal cannons stood almost wheel to wheel, with infantry in long lines in front and on either side. They all had a perfect target: massed Confederates wide and deep, wholly unprotected, every step taking them into better range of Union guns.

Lee's blind effort at victory lasted only forty minutes. Federal cannons ripped great gaps in the Southern ranks, while Northern infantry fired volley after volley into the thinning columns. Over 5,600 of Lee's men were killed or wounded. Of thirty-five high-ranking Confederate officers involved in the charge, only one escaped injury. Federals captured thirty of thirty-eight battle flags.

Below: One of the most horrible instances of the entire war was Lee's retreat from Gettysburg. Rain poured as a line of men and wagons extending for seventeen miles painfully made its way southward.

As survivors staggered back toward their lines Lee rode forward to meet them. He told Pickett: "This has been my fight and upon my shoulders rests the blame. The men and officers of your command have written the name of Virginia as high today as it has ever been written before."

Some of the beaten soldiers gathered around Lee. The general had difficulty in controlling his emotions. "You men have done all that men could do," he managed to say. "The fault is entirely my own."[9]

The three days of combat at Gettysburg consumed an unbelievable number of lives. One fourth of the Union army was killed, wounded, or missing. Lee lost more than one-third of the Army of Northern Virginia. Over 50,000 soldiers North and South had fallen in the battle.

Defeat at Gettysburg rested on Lee's shoulders. The first day's success caused him to continue the attacks. Yet the mistakes and might-have-beens by his corps commanders thereafter should have made Lee pause and think carefully about his next strategy.[10] At the same time, evidence exists that Lee was mentally and physically exhausted at the time of the battle. He simply was not up to fighting a major engagement not only without Jackson, but with inexperienced subordinates as well.[11]

On July 5 the Confederate army started home to Virginia in a pouring rain. Many of the men were barefooted. All were exhausted, hungry, and saddened at the outcome of the Northern invasion. Suddenly, Lee came riding along the slow-moving column. Weariness vanished as soldiers raised enthusiastic cheers: "Old Lee is still with us! Now all is well!" A Prussian officer riding with the army exclaimed: "I can truly say that nothing in the South touched and moved me more than the faithfulness of these thoroughly drenched, muddy, and ragged warriors to their noble leader in the disappointment of defeat."[12]

Never did the nobility of Robert E. Lee shine brighter than when he began his retreat from the Gettysburg battlefield. The general and his staff were making their way through rain down a crowded lane when a wounded Union soldier lying by the roadside saw the horsemen coming. Mustering as much strength as he could, the Federal shouted: "Hurrah for the Union!"

Lee heard the cry and reined Traveller to a halt. He dismounted and walked toward the soldier. The Billy Yank expected the officer to kill him. Instead, Lee took the man's hand, looked at him with genuine kindness, and said: "My son, I hope you will soon be well."

Such compassion from an enemy was overwhelming. "As soon as the general had left me," the wounded Federal confessed, "I cried myself to sleep there upon the bloody ground."[13]

Opposite: Every tourist visiting Gettysburg today stops at the Virginia Monument. Lee sits astride his horse, Traveller, while below him are Virginia soldiers from every walk of life.

Forced on the Defensive

THE ARMY RETURNED TO VIRGINIA WITH UNBROKEN FAITH IN LEE. NEWSPAPERS AND politicians were not as sympathetic. So strong became the criticisms that early in August, Lee asked President Davis to replace him with a "younger and abler" man. Lee expressed concern over how much confidence his army still had. In addition, he stated, "I sensibly feel the growing failure of my bodily strength. I have not yet recovered from the attack I experienced the past spring. I am becoming more and more incapable of exertion."[1]

Davis would hear none of it. Finding an abler general anywhere was impossible. Men of good sense and intelligence were behind Lee, Davis made clear.[2] Lee's soldiers didn't know about his offer to resign. Years later a veteran declared: "The army would have arisen in revolt if it had been called upon to give up General Lee."[3]

For the remainder of the summer of 1863, Lee undertook the slow task of rebuilding his weakened army in its position behind the Rapidan River. Making conditions worse was the deteriorating situation in the West. Federals were slowly occupying the state of Tennessee. Davis hoped that Lee might accept command in the West and take part of his army with him. Lee objected. He knew nothing of the Confederate Army of Tennessee or the western theater; and were he to leave Virginia, the Union Army of the Potomac would surely launch a new campaign. Davis and Lee reached a sort of compromise by Longstreet's corps being detached from Chattanooga, Tennessee.

General Meade also sent Union troops from his army to the Tennessee front. This move prompted Lee to go on the offensive. He led his men across the Rapidan and Rappahannock rivers in an attempt to turn Meade's right flank as he had turned Pope's army at Second Manassas. Unfortunately, A. P. Hill attacked too soon at Bristoe Station (October 14) and suffered heavy losses. Throughout those days, Lee was suffering so badly from back pains that he had to ride in a wagon.[4]

Lee pulled back. So did Meade. For six weeks the two forces jockeyed for position without any effect. Early in December both armies went into winter quarters.

Above: Civil War soldiers quickly learned that
whenever an army went into camp, digging
trenches and preparing earthworks were
the first order of business.

The break in the fighting brought little happiness to Lee. He saw the Confederacy slowly crumbling. The Mississippi valley was lost, as well as everything to the west of it. All of Tennessee was now in Union control, including the "Gateway to the Southeast": Chattanooga. Union blockade ships were tightening their hold on the Southern coastline. The northern half of Virginia was barren and scarred by war. At a time when the South needed unity in command, troops were being sent to every point of the Confederacy. No coordination existed. Lee's forces seemed to be all that stood between the Southern nation and defeat.

Winter weather in 1863–64 was severe. Clothing for the soldiers was as lacking as food. Unrepaired railroads and always-muddy roads blocked shipments of ample supplies. Late in January 1864, Lee informed the secretary of war: "Unless there is a change, I fear the army cannot be kept effective and probably cannot be kept together."[5]

Because of the hardships, or perhaps in spite of them, many soldiers spent the cold, blustery months getting closer to God. Religious revivals swept through the camps. Many brigades built log chapels where, night after night, chaplains and visiting missionaries preached salvation and eternity. An estimated 15,000 men were converted during the winter.[6]

Once in that period Lee went to Richmond for conversations with President Davis. He was able to visit his family in the Franklin Street home he had earlier leased for them. A shadow of sadness hung over the household. The Arlington mansion was lost forever. (Federals had seized the estate early in the war. Quartermaster General Montgomery Meigs showed his anger at Lee joining the Confederacy by ordering the property turned into a soldier cemetery. Hundreds of graves soon covered ground where once graceful trees and manicured fields had been.)

Mrs. Lee was now almost a helpless cripple because of arthritis. One son was in a soldier prison, a daughter was dead in a far-off cemetery, another child had been struck by tragedy because a rejected suitor had been killed, and Lee's only daughter-in-law was close to death. Lee was now aging noticeably. His hair and beard were snow white. A sharp pain regularly coursed through his left side.[7]

Morale in his army remained high throughout the bleak months. A major reason for this was Lee. He rode frequently among the camps and chatted with soldiers. Their needs were his constant concern. His admiration for his men was universally known. Their love for him was total. A Georgia private spoke for all when he wrote his wife: "I [can] look at him with his gray hair and beard only with feelings of awe and almost devotion."[8]

Many times in camp the story was told of Lee meeting a soldier coming from the battle line with a shattered right arm. "I grieve for you, my poor fellow," Lee said. "Can I do anything for you?"

The soldier replied: "Yes, sir, you can shake

Above: When Lee journeyed from the field of Richmond, Virginia, to confer with Jefferson Davis, the meeting took place at the presidential mansion downtown.

Robert E. Lee

hands with me, General, if you will consent to take my left hand."

Lee grasped the dirty hand warmly, making no attempt to hide the tears in his eyes.[9]

A few lighthearted moments broke the bleak winter period. No pets were available in Richmond, so Lee's teenage daughter, Mildred, caught and tried to tame a squirrel. The animal was named Custis Morgan after Mildred's oldest brother and the daring Kentucky raider who "will not stay in his cage." The squirrel was so unpredictable in behavior that it once bit Mrs. Lee's physician.

General Lee viewed the animal from afar with mock anger. Among his suggestions for the rodent was "squirrel soup thickened with peanuts." In that condition, Lee said, Custis Morgan "would cover himself with glory."

Nothing came of the suggestion because the squirrel slipped from the Lee home and disappeared. Yet the little animal provided the Lee family with several months of diversion from the heavy cares of war.[10]

Spring 1864 brought a renewal of battle. The odds against Lee were heavier than they had ever been. He could put 60,000 soldiers in the field, but he now could count on few

Opposite: **General U. S. Grant (1822-1885) was not impressive in appearance. Only five feet seven inches tall and weighing 135 pounds, he was a quiet commander who usually had a cigar in his mouth.**

replacements. Across the Rapidan, the Army of the Potomac was stronger, better disciplined, and better led than ever before. Meade still commanded the army. However, the Union's new general in chief, Ulysses S. Grant, intended to accompany that force and provide overall direction—as well as strength of will—to its operations.

Grant had won spectacular victories in the West. Lee had won the greater successes in the East. Now the best general each side had were to come face-to-face.

Lee braced himself. To his son Custis, he wrote: "Our country demands all our strength, all our energies. To resist the powerful combination now forming against us will require every man at his place. If victorious, we have everything to live for in the future. If defeated, nothing will be left for us to live for. . . . My whole trust is in God, and I am ready for whatever He may ordain."[11]

Grant's overall strategy was to send one Union force southward up the Shenandoah Valley and have another come at Richmond from the southeast. The principal thrust by the Army of the Potomac would be made against Lee. Grant told Meade: "Lee's army will be your objective point. Wherever Lee goes, there you will go also."[12]

And there would be no turning back. A courier brought Grant word that some pontoon bridges intended for the Rapidan River had been lost. Grant showed no concern. "If I beat General Lee," he declared, "I shan't want any pontoons; and if General Lee beats me, I can take all the men I intend to take back across the river on a log."[13]

On May 4 the Federal army began crossing the Rapidan. Accompanying the 122,000 Union soldiers were 274 cannons, 56,000 horses, 835 ambulance wagons, supply wagons that stretched for 25 miles, and thousands of cattle to be slaughtered along the way for fresh meat. Lee did not contest the crossing. He waited until Grant's divisions were locked amid the thick woods and along the narrow roads of the Wilderness. There Jackson had struck for victory a year earlier. There Lee struck again.

Two days of desperate fighting raged. Confederates gained the upper hand in the first day's action. A Union counterattack on May 6 pushed Lee's lines back almost to a breaking point. At the last moment Longstreet's badly needed corps rushed onto the field. Lee's anxiety turned to enthusiasm. He galloped up to Longstreet's lead unit, the Texas Brigade. "Hurrah for Texas!" Lee shouted. "Hurrah for Texas!"

The general then formed the men for a countercharge. As the Texans started forward they saw that Lee planned to lead the attack himself. "Go back, General Lee, go back!" the men shouted. "Lee to the rear! Lee to the rear!"

Lee continued to move forward on Traveller. The Texans slowed their pace. "Go back, General Lee!" the cries continued. "We won't go unless you go back!"

Seeing the intensity of the men, Lee reined his horse to a stop. The Texans then charged forward and broke the Union assault.[14]

The Wilderness was a victory for Lee. His soldiers had turned both Union flanks and inflicted 18,000 casualties while suffering 10,800 losses. In another sense, however, the Wilderness was not a Confederate success. Grant refused to withdraw—as McDowell, McClellan, Pope, and Hooker before him had done after defeat. Instead, Grant broke off the action and began advancing anew in an effort to turn Lee's right flank away from Richmond.

Confederates moved faster and made a new stand at the road junction of Spotsylvania Court House. Lee quickly ordered the construction of a four-mile line of field entrenchments. Johnny Rebs built earthworks, gun emplacements, and abatis (felled trees placed at angles designed to entangle attackers). Lee had become the "King of Spades" again, but no one was ridiculing him. By 1864 both armies had come to realize that "entrenchments were often the key to survival."[15]

A new phase in Lee's generalship was now beginning. He believed strongly in an attack as the best means of defense, but he lacked the manpower and resources to launch an offensive as long as Grant was willing to apply heavy pressure and to absorb heavy losses. Lee's strategy now was to conserve his forces and to wage skillful defense with the hope that time and his army would break the Northern will of a fight to the finish.

Starting on May 8, the opposing armies spent

Above: One of several representations
of the "Lee to the Rear" incident at
the Wilderness. The Texas troops
paid heavily that day for their valor.

Above: During the two-day struggle in the Wilderness, Confederates briefly seized a portion of the Union lines.

twelve days of intermittent but bitter combat around Spotsylvania. Lee was basically alone at his command post. Jeb Stuart was killed May 11 in a cavalry fight on the outskirts of Richmond; Longstreet had been wounded in the Wilderness; A. P. Hill was having bouts of illness; and Richard Ewell was so sick that he might collapse at any time. No veteran corps commander was at hand to offer Lee advice.

Grant soon discovered a weak point in Lee's Spotsylvania line. Because of the nature of the landscape, a full mile of Confederate works jutted forward in advance of Lee's main position. This salient was shaped like an inverted V. Rain was pouring on May 12 when Grant unloosed massive attacks against the salient. For seventeen hours some of the most violent fighting in history raged. Men grappled in hand-to-hand fighting while standing on dead and wounded soldiers.

The attacks at the "Bloody Angle" at first caught Lee by surprise. He dashed to the area and found his line about to snap. Reinforcements arrived. Lee was so relieved that he rode forward to lead them in a counterattack. Soldiers again stopped him by shouting: "Lee to the rear! Lee to the rear!"[16]

In the midst of rain and blood the Confederate line held. A Georgia regiment was moving up in support when one of the men saw Lee. "He was only a short distance in the rear, sitting on his horse with bared head, seemingly as cool and unexcited as a statue. The nobleness and majesty of his pose as he sat there, his bare head exposed to the rain of bursting shells, shrapnel, canister, minnie balls and falling limbs is a vivid picture which will never fade from my memory."[17]

When men were incapable of fighting any longer, the battle at Spotsylvania slowly ended. This action cost Grant another 18,000 men compared to 9,500 Confederates lost. It seemed as if Grant were hurling brigade after brigade to their deaths. Yet the Union commander knew what he was doing. He could fill the gaps in his ranks. Lee could not. Both generals were aware of this. At Spotsylvania one of Lee's officers remarked that Grant was throwing his men into battle like a butcher. Lee disagreed. "I think General Grant has managed his affairs remarkably well up to the present time," Lee said with little emotion. A few moments later Lee added wearily: "This army cannot stand a siege. We must end this business on the battlefield, not in a fortified place."[18]

Grant abandoned the Spotsylvania line and sidled eastward with the Union army toward the North Anna River. Lee anticipated such a move and shifted his own forces into defensive positions along the south bank of the river. On May 23 he narrowly missed being killed. Lee was resting on the front porch of a home overlooking the North Anna when a Union artillery officer across the way spotted the high-ranking Confederate. The artillerist fired a single round shot from one of his cannons. It passed within a few feet of Lee and embedded in the doorframe. Lee acted as if nothing had occurred.[19]

Illness struck Lee the next day. Perhaps it was a combination of long hours and bad food. For three days, as Confederates fought stubbornly to hold back Grant, "a violent intestinal complaint" kept Lee confined to his tent.[20]

The last days of May saw Grant swing south and east in yet another effort to make his way between Lee and Richmond. Lee continued to shift and remain in front of Grant. By the first of June, the Army of Northern Virginia was anchored along the Chickahominy River. Richmond was only nine miles away, but Lee had obtained reinforcements from the Shenandoah Valley and below Richmond. His army was strong, communications with Richmond were secure, and Lee's fortifications around the road junction of Cold Harbor were as powerful as Lee ever constructed.

That did not stop Grant from one more attempt to shatter the Confederate army. This time Grant ordered his divisions to make a head-on assault on the Southern fortifications. It was Fredericksburg all over again as one Union attack after another surged forward and was hurled back with heavy losses. Grant's casualties exceeded 7,000; Lee suffered only 1,500 losses. The bigger picture now was even more horrible for the North. From the Wilderness to Cold Harbor, Grant had suffered over 55,000 casualties. The Army of the Potomac was no closer to Richmond than McClellan had been two years earlier. For seventy miles and most of four weeks, the Confederates had

Above: No more vicious fighting occurred in the Civil War than on May 12, 1864, when there was hand-to-hand combat at Spotsylvania, Virginia. Only the width of the earthworks separated the two hosts.

been in constant contact with the enemy. Lee's defensive skills had been brilliant, as authorities on both sides agreed.

Still, Lee could take little pleasure in the situation. His own army had lost 32,000 men. This was a higher proportion of the army's size than Grant's losses had been. Further, Lee had suffered severely while winning battles. A few more such successes, and Lee's army would cease to exist.

In the past Confederates had always cheered great victories, but not now. The Southern ranks grew thinner with each battle. Union columns seemed always—even after defeat—to be endless. One Johnny Reb was heard muttering after Cold Harbor: "What's the use of killing these Yankees? It is like killing mosquitoes—two come for every one you kill."[21]

The condition of Lee's men was becoming frightful. A Confederate artillerist noted: "We had absolute faith in Lee's ability to meet and repel any assault . . . but there was an appalling and well-founded fear of starvation, which indeed some of us were already suffering. . . . In my own battery, three hard biscuits and one very meager slice of pork were . . . the first food that any of us had seen since our halt at the North Anna River two days before."[22]

At the same time, Grant's army was likely to lock Lee into a siege. That could end only in defeat for the Confederates. Time and lack of resources were now pressing hard against the South.[23] Unknown to Lee, Cold Harbor would be his last great victory in the field.

That is why Lee continued to seek an opportunity to attack and gain a decisive victory. On June 13 he dispatched one fourth of his army toward the Shenandoah Valley to clear that vital region of invaders. That same day the general learned of Grant's disappearance in front of him. The Union army sent up the James River in May toward Richmond had floundered badly and ended up doing nothing. Grant thereupon started a wide turning movement across the James River, around Richmond, and toward the vital rail junction of Petersburg, twenty miles south of the capital.

Grant's bold swing to the east caught Lee off guard. The Union army arrived before lightly defended Petersburg in plenty of time to capture the city and isolate Richmond.

Fortunately for Lee, the Union assaults were so poorly executed, and the Confederate defense so superbly made, that Lee and his army were able to reach Petersburg in time to block the main force of Grant's army. Nevertheless, Grant had Lee's force pinned down in the Petersburg earthworks.

Now the fate of the Army of Northern Virginia and Richmond and the Confederacy all became one and the same. The thing Lee most wished to avoid had now come to pass: a siege. Henceforth, a Confederate officer observed, "it was endurance without relief; sleeplessness without exhilaration; inactivity without rest; constant apprehension requiring ceaseless watching."[24]

From Siege to Defeat

History remembers Lee as a daring offensive commander. To do that is to forget that Lee was one of the greatest military engineers of the nineteenth century. His use of entrenchments was just as lasting a contribution to military science. Lee's field fortifications were magnificent at Fredericksburg, Spotsylvania, and Cold Harbor. To protect the Confederate capital, Lee constructed defensive works "of such depth and intricacy that they neutralized Grant's superior numbers" and insured that the Confederacy lived a year longer than it should have.[1]

The 1864–65 "siege of Richmond and Petersburg" is not an accurate phrase. In a true siege, a city is surrounded and cut off from food and other necessities. That never happened on the Richmond-Petersburg line. Yet conditions in Lee's army were almost as bad. Confederates had to defend miles of trenches. Murderous fire from sharpshooters, mortars, and long-range artillery occurred night and day.

All of this was a new and unpleasant experience for Lee. He had always won victories by shifting his army quickly and in unexpected directions. That kind of maneuver was no longer possible. The Army of Northern Virginia was on "a short chain." Lee could not move too far in any direction without risking Richmond, Petersburg, or one of the railroads so vital to the army's existence. Lee's greatest weapon in the past—mobility—was gone. He and his army were locked in the trenches. Hunger, filth, disease, exposure to the elements, constant fire from the enemy, and desertion would slowly sap the strength from "Lee's Miserables," as many termed themselves.[2]

Lee was helpless to change events. His pleas for food, clothing, and more men brought no more response than had George Washington's anguished calls from Valley Forge. Lee could only watch as Federals occupied the Shenandoah Valley, secured the piedmont section of northern Virginia, seized Atlanta, and cut the Confederacy in two with General William T. Sherman's "March to the Sea." All of this put Lee in a sort of vacuum. He needed help, and there was none.

His military sense told him that Richmond could no longer be defended. The city had become a great weight on his shoulders.

Above: **The second of two Union divisions charging the Confederate lines at the point of "The Crater." Lack of coordination on the Union side, plus angry determination by the Confederates, turned the battle into a Southern victory.**

Confederate soldiers needed to get in the open in order to have a chance for victory. Yet Lee the Southerner realized that the loss of Richmond would have a paralyzing, if not fatal, effect on what was left of the Confederate nation. To give up the city without a fight would also make Lee a traitor in the eyes of many of his countrymen.

Within a week after arriving at Petersburg, Lee sent a personal letter to President Davis. Lee admitted for the first time that he did not expect victory in the war. "Genl. Grant will concentrate all the troops here he can raise, from every section of the U.S. . . . The enemy is . . . so situated that I cannot attack him."[3]

Nine grinding, weakening months under siege followed. Lee conducted the longest sustained defensive operation of the Civil War at Petersburg. His 66,000 Confederates manned a 45-mile line and faced over 112,000 Union soldiers. Never was there a day without casualties. The only breaks in daily Federal artillery bombardments were battles. They generally were fought for control of the railroads from the south that were Lee's supply lines and Richmond's lifelines.

Grant's strategy was simple: to extend his lines west, forcing Lee to do the same with his thin forces. Late June brought fighting along the Weldon Railroad. On July 30, Grant switched tactics and attacked Lee's lines in front of Petersburg by novel means. A regiment of Union coal miners dug a 511-foot tunnel from their lines to beneath the Confederate earthworks. At the end of the mine Federals placed 8,000 pounds of gunpowder. The spectacular explosion at 4:45 a.m. blew a hole 170 feet long, 60 feet wide, and 30 feet deep.

Two Union divisions assaulted amid the smoke and confusion. The Federals lacked sufficient leadership, and the Southerners counterattacked with cold fury. The "Battle of the Crater" cost Grant 4,000 men. Lee's losses were barely one-third of that number. After the battle, Grant made no move on Petersburg itself. Rather, he concentrated on maneuvering Lee into the open by probes and major field attacks.

With August came battle at Globe Tavern on the Weldon Railroad. Union losses were high, but Grant succeeded in cutting the line. The next two months saw sharp engagements at Peeble's Farm and Hatcher's Run. Confederates were able to maintain their positions in the face of heavy casualties on both sides.

Abraham Lincoln's reelection in November over a peace-movement Democrat was a clear signal that the war would be fought to the end, with no compromise. Heavy desertions began from Lee's ranks. Lee recalled most of the Confederates left in the Shenandoah Valley to the Richmond-Petersburg line. This move marked the end of Lee's efforts to maintain a workable second front.

In December, Federals struck Hickford and destroyed another sixteen miles of railroad. A Union attempt to secure the Boydton Plank Road, one of the last remaining Confederate supply routes, failed as Lee's men fought desperately. By late winter Lee's army was badly extended and near exhaustion. Lee made a personal appeal for help. He later told his son: "Well, I have been up to see the Congress and they do not seem to be able to do anything except to eat peanuts and chew tobacco, while my army is starving."[4]

Lee was able to conceal melancholy feelings from his soldiers. "His countenance seldom, if ever, exhibited the least traces of anxiety," a staff officer noted, "but was firm, hopeful, and encouraged those around him in the belief that he was still confident of success." The writer added: "The troops followed him with their eyes, or their cheers, whenever he appeared, feeling a singular sense of confidence from the presence of the gray-haired soldier in his plain uniform, and assured that, as long as Lee led them, the cause was safe."[5]

Throughout the long dreary winter, Lee alone held fast against Union might. The Confederate Congress passed an act creating the position of general in chief. Lee was the obvious person for the job. President Davis considered the bill a vote of no confidence in his leadership, but he swallowed his pride and signed the measure into law.

The appointment came too late to be meaningful. For example, early in January 1865, Lee came out in favor of a most revolutionary proposal: to use slaves as soldiers. When such a bill was introduced in Congress, Lee wrote one of the sponsors that the act was vital for the survival of the Confederacy. "We must decide whether slavery shall be extinguished by our enemies, and the slaves used against us, or use them ourselves at the risk of the effects which may be produced upon our social institutions. My own opinion is that we should employ them without delay."

At the same time, Lee added, the slaves themselves ought to get something in return if they were going to fight. "The Negroes, under proper circumstances, will make efficient soldiers. . . . Those who are employed should be freed. It would be neither just nor wise . . . to require them to serve as slaves."[6]

Nothing of note came from Lee's proposals. No organized unit of Confederate black troops saw action in the field.

By the end of March, snows had turned to rain and temperatures were climbing. Soon the roads would be dry, Lee knew, and Grant's army would move. Federals began massing in strength against the Confederate right for an offensive. Lee rushed as many soldiers as he could spare to the flank ten miles southwest of Petersburg. He was able to get 12,000 men in line. On March 31, in a struggle fought in mud after a thirty-six-hour downpour, the Confederates were beaten back by a turning force of 53,000 Federals. Lee sent a desperate message to the commanders at the vital road junction in that area: "Hold Five Forks at all hazards."[7]

The next day Grant broke Lee's lines at Five Forks. In two disastrous hours the units that Lee had painfully assembled to protect his southwestern flank were so swept away that they virtually ceased to exist. Some 3,000 Southerners were captured in addition to those killed and wounded. The Union army now stood poised to sweep around Lee's flank and slash the two remaining Confederate railroads.

Lee's defenses by then were little more than a heavy skirmish line in the main earthworks. At midnight that Saturday, April 1, Union artillery along the entire front began the heaviest bombardment of the war. Shell bursts and flashes from mortars and rockets lit the dark sky. The earth shook for miles under the swelling roar of continuous explosions.

With the dawn of April 2, Grant struck with his full army. One corps smashed through A. P. Hill's defenses southwest of Petersburg and killed the popular general in the first fighting. Lee himself almost fell captive as his lines crumbled under the weight of Union numbers.

The long-awaited disaster had occurred. Lee fell back to the inner ring of Petersburg defenses and sent word to Richmond that his lines were broken. He must abandon the Richmond-Petersburg position that night and seek a new line elsewhere. Throughout the growing disaster of that day, Lee's composure remained steady. His chief of staff, Colonel Walter Taylor, stated:

Above: **The village of Appomattox Court House, looking east. The McLean home is at the far right.**

"Self-contained and serene, he acted as one who was conscious of having accomplished all that was possible in the line of duty. . . . There was no apparent excitement and no sign of apprehension as he issued his orders for the retreat of his sadly reduced army. . . . It was a striking illustration of Christian fortitude."[8]

Lee had done everything he could in the long nine months at Petersburg. Against superior manpower and armament, he had stood firm while every misfortune and hardship whittled away at his gallant band. Lee had inflicted

42,000 enemy casualties, but his own forces had suffered 28,000 losses. Lee had led and inspired; he had begged for help and prayed for guidance; he had employed every ounce of his talents and given the Southern cause every hour of his time. In the end, he had failed because no mortal could have succeeded under the circumstances.

So quietly did the Confederates evacuate Petersburg that Lee stole a day's march on Grant. The retreat was due west toward the Richmond and Danville Railroad. At the depot of Amelia, Lee's men would unite with the Richmond defenders. Food supplies would supposedly be waiting there. The combined force would then move southwest along the railroad toward the hilly city of Danville, where a strong defense could be established.

Nothing seemed to go right for the tired and hungry Southern army. The train from Danville with food passed through Amelia for some reason and proceeded to Richmond—and was captured by Union soldiers. Lee had to spend a day hunting for rations in the Amelia area. This gave Grant time to get Union cavalry in front of Lee. Federal horsemen cut the Richmond and Danville line at Jetersville. Lee had to turn west in the direction of Lynchburg and the Southside Railroad.

Grant's army pursued Lee doggedly. Union cavalry nipped at the columns at every opportunity. What was left of the Army of Northern Virginia trudged slowly westward. Signs of defeat were everywhere—broken-down wagons and caissons, abandoned equipment, discarded weapons. Starved horses slowly sank to the ground. Some were hitched, while others could no longer hold their riders. Many soldiers simply sat along the roadside, too tired or dejected to keep going. Others marched on, out of a sense of habit or loyalty.

Near the end of Lee's column a hungry North Carolina soldier poked among the bushes in search of a rabbit or squirrel. Suddenly, he found himself surrounded by Union soldiers. "Surrender! We've got you!" one Billy Yank shouted.

The Carolinian dropped his musket and raised his hands. "Yes," he said, "you've got me. And a hell of a git you've got!"[9]

For six days the army stumbled along dirt roads. The pace slowed with each passing day. Thirst, hunger, weariness, sore feet, aching muscles, sagging spirits—all bled Lee's army. Meanwhile, Grant slowly closed the gap. By Sunday morning, April 9, the Union army had surrounded what was left of Lee's forces. At long last the "Gray Fox" (as Lee was often called) had been brought to bay.

Lee made a number of memorable statements that fateful Palm Sunday.

Early in the morning General Porter Alexander visited Lee. The brilliant artillerist suggested that Lee not surrender. Rather, he should order all Confederates to scatter to the hills and byways. Conduct guerrilla warfare throughout the South for as long as it took the North to grow tired of it and quit the war. This is the way most civil wars run their course.

***Below:* Lee's meeting with Grant lasted three hours. A single officer accompanied Lee, while a sizable escort of Union officers stood behind Grant.**

Lee rejected Alexander's ideas. The few thousand soldiers who escaped, Lee said, could not change the outcome of the struggle. What guerrilla warfare would produce would not be victory for the South, but disaster for all of America. "Already [the country] is demoralized by the four years of war," Lee declared. "If I took your advice, the men would be without rations and under no control of officers. They would be compelled to rob and steal in order to live. . . . We would bring in a state of affairs it would take the country years to recover from." Besides, Lee confessed, he was too old and too tired to begin a new war of bushwhacking.[10] That was the last mention of guerrilla warfare in Lee's presence.

It was soon obvious that surrender was the

only course left. "There is nothing left for me to do but to go and see General Grant," Lee told an aide, "and I would rather die a thousand deaths."[11]

For a moment Lee thought of a simple way out. He looked at the massed Federal lines at his front and said: "How easily I could be rid of this, and be at rest! I have only to ride along the lines and all will be over."

He had followed his conscience to the end, but by then the general was scarcely able to control his feelings. Yet he sighed, drew himself erect, and exclaimed: "But it is our duty to live. What will become of the women and children of

Above: **Grown men who had served and suffered through years of combat wept openly when Lee returned to his lines and announced the surrender of the Southern army.**

the South if we are not here to protect them?"[12]

The meeting with Grant began early in the afternoon at Wilmer McLean's home across the road from the Appomattox Court House. Grant had known more than his share of failing in life. He sought to put Lee at ease and, as much as he could, soften the weight of the blow that was about to fall. "My own feelings," Grant later wrote, "were sad and depressed. I felt like anything rather than rejoicing at the downfall of a foe who had fought so long and valiantly, and suffered so much for a cause."[13]

Drafting the surrender document took two hours. Grant was generous in his terms. Officers would be allowed to keep their sidearms, and cavalrymen could take their mounts home for the spring plowing. Confederates who laid down their weapons would receive pardons. As long as they obeyed the law, they were not to be disturbed by any Union authorities. Grant even ordered thousands of rations issued at once to starving soldiers who, until that moment, had been the enemy.

Federal displays of respect at Appomattox showed clearly that honor rather than humiliation would be the starting point for a new nation. Johnny Rebs never apologized for what they had done, and Billy Yanks never asked them to do so.

Lee concluded the meeting with Grant and rode slowly back to deliver the difficult news to his waiting army. Ragged soldiers swarmed around their commander and cheered. Lee spoke to them from the saddle. "Men, we have fought the war together, and I have done the best I could for you. You will all be paroled and go to your homes until exchanged." At that point Lee's eyes filled with tears. His throat tightened. A broken "good-bye" was all he could say.[14]

Hundreds of men began weeping, while others poured out their affection for Lee even more intensely. One dirty Confederate, now aware that the war was over, reached up and shouted: "I love you just as well as ever, General Lee!"[15]

The following day Lee issued a farewell order to his army. He praised the "unsurpassed courage and fortitude" of the men and asked God's blessing and protection for them in the days that lay ahead. The final words of General Order No. 9 read: "With an unceasing admiration of your constancy and devotion to your country, and a grateful remembrance of your kind and generous consideration for myself, I bid you an affectionate farewell."[16]

A defeated and downcast general then pointed Traveller toward Richmond and his family. The North had victory; the South now had only Lee.

Opposite: Lee sat on the back porch on his temporary Richmond, Virginia, home for this photograph, taken less than a week after the events at Appomattox. The strains of war are clearly evident in Lee's features.

National Symbol **10**

LEE RETURNED TO A CAPITAL IN ASHES. CONFEDERATE OFFICIALS WERE ABANDONING Richmond on the night of April 2–3 when the flames of military supplies set afire raged out of control and swept through the city. The entire downtown area was destroyed. Symbolically, Richmond went up in flames with the Confederacy.

Lee headed toward the Franklin Street home where his family had resided for most of the war. It had barely survived flames that had swept to within a block. As Lee rode across the pontoon bridge into Richmond early in the morning, large crowds of silent Virginians, Union soldiers, and dislocated blacks gathered along the route. "There was no excitement, no hurrahing," one eyewitness noted, "but as the great chief passed, a deep, loving murmur, greater than these, rose from the very heart of the crowd. Taking off his hat, and simply bowing his head, the man great in adversity passed silently to his own door; it closed upon him; and his people had seen him for the last time in his battle harness."[1]

He had no job or income. His beloved Virginia had been destroyed. Desolation and poverty were upon the land. Lee was exhausted in mind and body. Perhaps he felt that the sorrows of the whole South were his burden.

From the day of surrender, Lee concluded to remain in Virginia. The state offered little for the future. Yet for Lee, Virginia was home. He told a friend: "Now, more than at any other time, Virginia and every state in the South needs us. We must try and, with as little delay as possible, go to work and build up their prosperity." Lee also declined an invitation to visit Europe for an extended stay. "I cannot desert my native state in the hour of her adversity," he stated. "I must abide her fortune, and share her fate."[2]

There was no bitterness in defeat. Lee was above that. "All should unite," he declared, "in honest efforts to obliterate the effects of war, and to restore the blessings of peace."[3] Lee determined to set the example himself.

He regularly attended services at St. Paul's Episcopal Church in Richmond. Some blacks came to the services, but the seating was segregated. One Sunday the minister invited the faithful to come forth and receive communion

Photo-FOSTER

Left: In 1864 the Lee family had leased this home on East Franklin Street in Richmond, Virginia. Lee resided there for two months following the war.

Above: **By war's end, Mrs. Lee was a bitter invalid. Her husband proved ever caring in his attention to her.**

at the chancel railing. A well-dressed black man walked forward. The congregation seemed to freeze. The man knelt alone at the railing—until Lee walked calmly from his pew and knelt beside him. The congregation quickly followed suit.[4]

By summer Lee was anxious to leave Richmond. The city was too full of people, noise, and confusion. He wanted to buy some land in the country, move there, and try to live the quiet life of a retired farmer. Mrs. Elizabeth Randolph Cocke, a wealthy widow, invited the Lees to occupy a small house on her James River estate above Richmond. The home, named Derwent, was not elaborate, but it was adequate. For two months Lee and his family enjoyed the solitude.

Meanwhile, trustees at Washington College in Lexington were seeking a president. They had precious little to offer. The school had been a small, respectable college at the southern end of the Shenandoah Valley. In 1864, Federal soldiers had ransacked the campus, scattered the library, destroyed laboratory equipment, and left the buildings heavily damaged. Its previous students had mostly joined the army. Only forty-five male students and four faculty members remained.

The trustees needed a prominent person at the head for fund-raising. So poor was the place that Judge John W. Brockenbrough, rector of the Board of Trustees, had to borrow a suit of clothes and fifty dollars to ride to Derwent and offer the position to Lee.

Lee hesitated. The position offered neither fortune nor fame. His previous academic experience as superintendent at West Point had not been a pleasant time. Lee also knew that many in the North regarded him as a traitor and the most dangerous of all the ex-Confederates. Such feelings would not be helpful for the school.

The encouragement of friends was a factor in Lee's decision. So were sentiments he later explained in a letter to his wife. "Life is indeed gliding away and I have nothing of good to show for mine that is past. I pray I may be

Below: **During the Lexington years, Lee would often mount Traveller for an afternoon ride through the countryside. The beloved horse lived only two years following Lee's death.**

Robert E. Lee

spared to accomplish something for the benefit of mankind and to the honour of God."[5]

Lee accepted the offer to become a college president. He informed the trustees: "I think it is the duty of every citizen, in the present condition of the Country, to do all in his power to aid in the restoration of peace and harmony. . . . It is particularly incumbent on those charged with the instruction of the young to set them an example of submission to authority."[6] Lee stated his personal feelings in simple terms. "I have a self-imposed task which I must accomplish. I have led the young men of the South in battle; I have seen many of them die on the field; I shall devote my remaining energies to training young men to do their duty in life."[7]

In mid-September, Lee arrived in Lexington and assumed his new post. He recalled West Point and how everything there was organized and everyone was part of a distinct chain of command. Now, at Washington College, Lee held a blank sheet of paper and looked at confusion and uncertainty. Yet he instantly showed that he would be a hands-on president, not a figurehead. One of his first tasks was to review the qualities of each faculty member and to interview personally each student.

Contributions flowed into the school from admirers of Lee. Former abolitionist Henry Ward Beecher raised funds. Cyrus McCormick, inventor of the first grain reaper only a few miles from Lexington, was a leading contributor. Over $100,000 had been received by the end of Lee's first presidential year. The faculty increased from four to fourteen, while enrollment doubled to more than 100 students. Lee established ten areas of study, liberalized the overall curriculum, laid the groundwork for a law school, and watched with pleasure the construction of a campus chapel.

He also introduced an "honor code" of behavior whereby he "treated the students as gentlemen and expected them to act as gentlemen."[8] Lee's discipline of "my boys" (as he called the students) consisted of a fatherly talk rather than a customary paddling. A student called before Lee for misconduct later confessed: "I wish he had whipped me. I could have stood it better. But he talked to me so kindly, and so tenderly, about my mother, and the sacrifices which she, a widow, is making to send me to college, and of how I ought to appreciate her love . . . that the first thing I knew I was blubbering like a baby."[9]

Few college presidents ever worked harder for the religious good of the students. To one local minister, Lee said: "I shall fail in the leading object that brought me here, unless these young men become real Christians." He repeated similar thoughts to another clergyman: "I dread the thought of any student going away from the College without becoming a sincere Christian."[10]

At the same time, Lee silenced many of his Northern enemies by twice testifying before congressional committees in Washington. At one point he accepted an invitation for a brief meeting with Grant, now president, in the White House. Lee was always ready to give counsel on the future to former Confederates. The advice never varied: Forget the passions of the past, and live in peace as loyal Americans.

When Lee applied for a pardon, he was unaware that an oath of allegiance had to be taken by all former Confederate officers. Shortly after the war Lee signed an oath and mailed it to Washington. The government, for unknown reasons, never acknowledged receipt. The mistake was not discovered until 1975, and Congress granted Lee a pardon.

The Washington College years were not especially happy ones for the general. "Traveller is my only companion," Lee observed. "I may also say my pleasure. He and I, whenever practicable, wander out in the mountains and enjoy sweet confidence."[11] Occasionally, those short trips took him to the Lexington cemetery. There Lee would stand in thought beside the grave of his great lieutenant, Thomas "Stonewall" Jackson.

His health was slowly failing, his wife's arthritic condition was totally crippling, and the struggle to resurrect the college from the ashes of war was both long and tedious. If happiness was not there for Lee, a sense of fulfillment was.

He was doing his duty, which now was to educate the young rather than lead them into battle.

His confidence rested on history. He wrote Colonel Charles Marshall, his wartime aide: "The truth is this: The march of Providence is so slow and our desires so impatient; the work of progress is so immense and our means of aiding it so feeble; the life of humanity is so long, [and] that of the individual so brief, that we often see only the ebb of the advancing wave and are thus discouraged. It is history that teaches each of us to hope."[12]

Lee continually impressed everyone who saw him. He refused to use liquor, tobacco, or profanity. He was such a doting father that none of his three surviving daughters ever married. Esteemed as a model Southerner, Lee was always in demand at functions. Yet he shunned large gatherings and public acclaim.

In 1867 the Radical Republican–controlled Congress placed the South under military occupation. "Reconstruction" thus began. Lee again took the lead in advising peace and dignity rather than anger and revenge. A Confederate widow voiced deep hatred for all Yankees. The commander who had led armies against the North replied calmly: "Madam, do not

Opposite: **This is supposedly the last photograph of Lee. He was sixty-three years old and in rapidly declining health.**

Above: The funeral and burial of Lee were at the chapel on the college campus. Part of the crowd attending the service stands outside on the unusually warm day.

train your children in hostility to the government of the United States. Remember, we are all one country now. Dismiss from your mind all sectional feeling, and bring them up to be Americans."[13]

Possibly the most startling event of Lee's postwar years came in 1868, when the *New York Herald* endorsed Lee for president of the United States. The newspaper did so on the grounds that Lee was a better man in every way than Republican candidate Ulysses S. Grant. Lee ignored the matter, as he did all politics.

Washington College grew steadily in both size and prestige. The campus filled with 20 professors and 400 students. Yet the strain of war had been too great for Lee's strong heart. Soon after the 1869–70 school year began, the general's heart ailment became more pronounced. He was in bed for several days. Once back at his duties, Lee began to experience difficulty in breathing. His condition grew so serious that the faculty begged him to take a vacation.

The spring 1870 trip through the Deep South was done presumably for his health, but it was more likely a farewell tour. Lee sensed that he was dying. He visited old scenes and old friends of earlier years. He even agreed to sit for a portrait and pose for a statue.

Another school year began in September. Lee was only sixty-three years old, but he appeared aged with snow-white hair, a slight stoop, slowness in walking, and always seemed tired. The general was attempting to say grace at dinner on September 28 when he suffered a paralyzing stroke. At 9:30 a.m. on October 12 the painful breathing ceased. Robert Lee's earthly campaigns were done.

His death brought national mourning. A New York City newspaper, with every reason to damn Lee forevermore, stated at his passing: "In him the military genius of America was developed in a greater extent than ever before. In him all that was pure and lofty in mind and purpose found lodgment. He came nearer the ideal of a soldier and Christian general than any man we can think of."[14]

Hundreds of eulogies appeared in every corner of the land. None was more moving, or more simple, than that from Julia Ward Howe. The Northern lady who had sent Union soldiers confidently into battle with the words of "The Battle Hymn of the Republic" wrote of Lee:

A gallant foeman in the fight,
A brother when the fight was o'er,
The hand that led the host with might
The blessed torch of learning bore. . . .
Thought may the minds of men divide,
Love makes the heart of nations one,
And so, thy soldier grave beside,
We honor thee, Virginia's son.[15]

Lee's remains were buried in the college chapel. Trustees quickly changed the name of the school from Washington College to Washington and Lee University. To this day, however, many of its graduates refer to it as "General Lee's College."

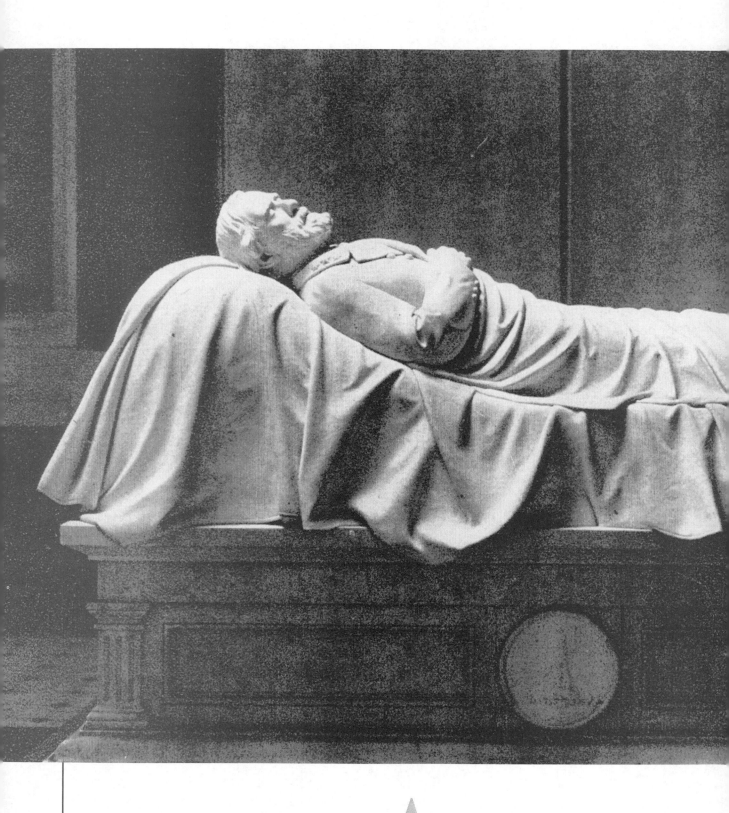

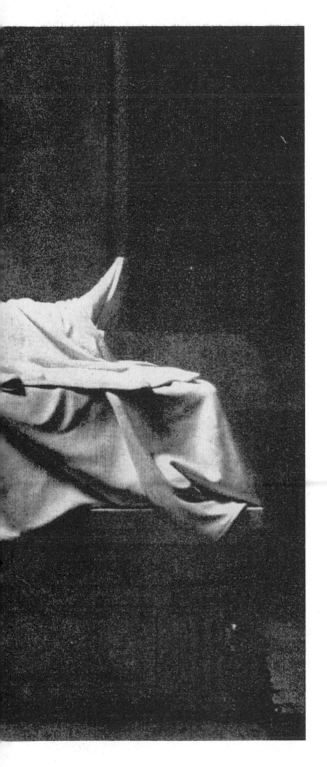

Left: **Few monuments are more moving than the Edward V. Valentine sculpture of a uniformed Lee presumably asleep in his tent. The statue is directly above Lee's tomb in the chapel's basement.**

Five years as a college president may well stand as the crowning achievement of Lee's life. A terrible civil war had fractured America, and the wounds seemed too deep for any healing. Half of the American nation stood in the humiliation of defeat. Then Lee stepped forward. The general, one writer summarized, "was the only man who had the chance to do it all—save the South's pride, give the South the calm example that would guide it in a stormy postwar period, and do it all in a way that the North would first approve and then applaud."[16]

Lee was forced to make imperfect choices in an imperfect world. Great in war, greater after war, Lee asked no pardon for doing any wrong. He was a man seemingly always at peace with himself, whether it was in leading soldiers into legend or carrying a nation into the dawn of a new day.

Notes

INTRODUCTION

1. Charles Marshall, *An Aide-de-Camp of Lee* (Boston: Little, Brown, 1922), p. 173.

2. Charles P. Roland, *Reflections on Lee: An Assessment* (Mechanicsburg, PA: Stackpole Books, 1993), p. 1. Lee and his great lieutenant, "Stonewall" Jackson, have been commemorated on U.S. postage stamps—an honor never bestowed on any other individuals who led armies against this country.

3. Garnet J. W. Wolseley, *The Story of a Soldier's Life* (Westminster, England: A. Constable, 1903), vol. 2; p. 135.

4. Charles Francis Adams, *Three Phi Beta Kappa Lectures* (Boston: Houghton Mifflin, 1907), pp. 96–97.

Chapter 1: The Making of a Soldier

1. Albert Marrin, *Virginia's General: Robert E. Lee and the Civil War* (New York: Atheneum, 1994), p. 7.

2. Stanley F. Horn, ed., *The Robert E. Lee Reader* (New York: Grossett & Dunlap, 1949), p. 15.

3. Douglas Southall Freeman, *R. E. Lee: A Biography* (New York: Charles Scribner's Sons, 1934-35), vol. 1, p. 9.

4. Paul C. Nagel, *The Lees of Virginia* (New York: Oxford University Press, 1990), p. 166.

5. Alonzo T. Dill and Mary Tyler Cheek, *A Visit to Stratford and the Story of the Lees* (Stratford, VA: Stratford Hall Foundation, 1986), pp. 16–17.

6. A. L. Long, *Memoirs of Robert E. Lee* (New York: J. M. Stoddard, 1886), p. 71.

7. Clifford Dowdey, *Lee* (Boston: Little, Brown, 1965), p. 46.

8 At the head of the class was New Yorker Charles Mason. He taught engineering at West Point for two years, resigned to become a lawyer, and eventually rose to chief justice of the Iowa Supreme Court.

9. Douglas Southall Freeman, *Lee of Virginia* (New York: Charles Scribner's Sons, 1958), p. 22.

10. Freeman, *R. E. Lee*, vol. 1, pp. 173–74.

11. Ibid., vol. 1, p. 156.

12. Freeman, *Lee of Virginia*, p. 25.

13. Freeman, *R. E. Lee*, vol. 1, p. 203.

14. Emory M. Thomas, *Robert E. Lee: A Biography* (New York: W. W. Norton, 1995), p. 121.

15. Freeman, *R. E. Lee*, vol. 1, p. 229.

16. Ibid., vol. 1 pp. 239–40.

17. Al Kaltman, *The Genius of Robert E. Lee* (Paramus, NJ: Prentice-Hall, 2000), p. 63.

18. Freeman, *R. E. Lee*, vol. 1, p. 272.

19. Ibid., vol. 1, p. 280; Dowdey, *Lee*, pp. 93–94.

20. Allan R. Millett and Peter Maslowski, *For the Common Defense: A Military History of the United States of America* (New York: Free Press, 1984), p. 149.

21. Richard S. Ewell to Benjamin P. Ewell, November 17, 1847, Richard Stoddard Ewell Papers, Library of Congress.

22. Freeman, *R. E. Lee*, vol. 1, p. 294.

23. Ibid.

24. J. William Jones, *Life and Letters of Robert Edward Lee, Soldier and Man* (New York: Neale, 1906), p. 53

Chapter 2: Nation Versus Country

1. Robert E. Lee Jr., *Recollections and Letters of General Robert E. Lee* (New York: Doubleday Page, 1904), pp. 8–9.

2. Freeman, *R. E. Lee*, vol. 1, p. 321.

3. Kaltman, *Genius of Lee*, p. 88.

4. Ibid., 94.

5. Freeman, *R. E. Lee*, vol. 1, pp. 330–31. See also Lee, *Recollections*, p. 106.

6. John Esten Cooke, *A Life of General Robert E. Lee* (New York: D. Appleton, 1871), p. 558.

7. Freeman, *R. E. Lee*, vol. 1, p. 378.

8. Horn, *Lee Reader*, p. 79.

9. Freeman, *R. E. Lee*, vol. 1, p. 372; Thomas, *Robert E. Lee*, p. 173.

10. Freeman, *R. E. Lee*, vol. 1, p. 400; Freeman, *Lee of Virginia*, p. 50.

11. Jones, *Life and Letters*, p. 119.

12. Ibid., p. 121. At the same time, Lee borrowed words from the Bible in a letter to his son Custis: "The country seems to be in a lamentable condition. . . . May God rescue us from the folly of our own acts, save us from unselfishness and teach us to love our neighbors as ourselves" (Ibid., p. 122).

13. Abraham Lincoln, *The Collected Works of Abraham Lincoln* (New Brunswick, NJ: Rutgers University Press, 1953–55), vol. 4 (1953), p. 332.

14. The home still stands on Pennsylvania Avenue across the street from the White House. Blair House today is used for foreign heads of state who come to visit the president.

15. Lee, *Recollections*, p. 27.

16. Freeman, *R. E. Lee*, vol. 1, p. 437.

17. Ibid.

18. Roland, *Reflections*, p. 22.

19. Robert E. Lee, *The Wartime Papers of R. E. Lee* (Boston: Little, Brown, 1961), p. 11.

20. *Journals and Papers of the Virginia State Convention of 1861* (Richmond: Virginia State Library, 1961–66), vol. 1 (1961), p. 188. A statue of Lee is on the spot in the capitol where he assumed command.

Chapter 3: Rocky Path to Army Command

1. Mary Boykin Chesnut, *Mary Chesnut's Civil War* (New Haven, CT: Yale University Press, 1981), pp. 54–55.

2. Freeman, *R. E. Lee*, vol. 1, p. 450n.

3. Kaltman, *Genius of Lee*, p. 134.

4. Roland, *Reflections*, p. 27; Freeman, *Lee of Virginia*, p. 62.

5. Walter H. Taylor, *General Lee: His Campaigns in Virginia, 1861–1865* (Brooklyn, NY: Braunsworth & Co., 1906), pp. 24–25.

6. Charles T. Quintard, *Doctor Quintard, Chaplain, C.S.A.* (Sewanee, TN: The University Press, 1905), p. 17.

7. Freeman, *Lee of Virginia*, p. 64.

8. Freeman, *R. E. Lee*, vol. 2, p. 564.

9. Isaac Noyes Smith, "A Virginian's Dilemma," West Virginia History 27 (1965–66): pp. 183–84.

10. Freeman, *R. E. Lee*, vol. 2, pp. 552–53.

11. David L. Phillips, *War Diaries: The 1861 Kanawha Valley Campaigns* (Leesburg, VA: Gauley Mount Press, 1990), p. 438.

12. Lee, *Wartime Papers*, p. 80.

13. Kaltman, *Genius of Lee*, p. 161.

14. For the acquisition and the character of Traveller, see Freeman, *R. E. Lee*, vol. 1, pp. 615, 644–47.

15. Freeman, *Lee of Virginia*, p. 68.

16. Lee, *Wartime Papers*, p. 122.

17. Roland, *Reflections*, p. 35.

18. U.S. War Department, comp., *War of the Rebellion: A Compilation of the Official Records of the Union and Confederate Armies* (Washington, DC: Government Printing Office, 1880–1901), Ser. I, vol. 5, p. 1099. Cited hereafter as *Official Records*; unless otherwise stated, all references will be to Ser. I.

19. Lee, *Wartime Papers*, pp. 127–28.

20. Freeman, *R. E. Lee*, vol. 1, pp. 602, 607.

21. Marshall, *Aide-de-Camp*, p. 32.

22. Freeman, *R. E. Lee*, vol. 2, p. 48. Postmaster General John Reagan, who recorded this incident, later wrote that he never saw Lee exhibit so much emotion as at that moment.

23. Contrary to popular belief, the Confederacy's major army was called the Army of Northern Virginia months before Lee took command of it (Freeman, *R. E. Lee*, vol. 2, p. 77n).

24. The nickname even made it into book titles; see John H. Worsham, *One of Jackson's Foot Cavalry* (New York: Neale, 1912).

Chapter 4: Brilliance in the Field

1. *Richmond Examiner*, June 17, 1862.

2. George B. McClellan, *The Civil War Papers of*

George B. McClellan (New York: Ticknor & Fields, 1989), pp. 244–45.

3. Jefferson Davis, *The Rise and Fall of the Confederate Government* (New York: D. Appleton, 1881), vol. 2, p. 127.

4. E. Porter Alexander, *Fighting for the Confederacy: The Personal Recollections of Edward Porter Alexander* (Chapel Hill: University of North Carolina Press, 1989), p. 91.

5. Lee, *Wartime Papers*, 184.

6. R. U. Johnson and C. C. Buel, eds., *Battles and Leaders of the Civil War* (New York: Century Company, 1887–88), vol. 2, p. 394.

7. See John M. Taylor, *Duty Faithfully Performed: Robert E. Lee and His Critics* (Dulles, VA: Brassey's, 1999), pp. 77–78.

8. *Southern Historical Society Papers* (Richmond: Southern Historical Society, 1876–1952), vol. 4 (1877), p. 274.

9. John O. Casler, *Four Years in the Stonewall Brigade* (Dayton, OH: Morningside Bookshop, 1977), p. 103.

10. Marrin, *Virginia's General*, p. 74.

11. William Dorsey Pender, *The General to His Lady* (Chapel Hill: University of North Carolina Press, 1962), p. 171.

12. Long, *Memoirs*, p. 112.

Chapter 5: The Bloodiest Day

1. Lee, *Wartime Papers*, p. 293.

2. Freeman, *R. E. Lee*, vol. 2, p. 340. The entire Confederate high command was hurting in the Maryland campaign. Jackson had been thrown from a horse and had to ride for a few days in a carriage. Longstreet, hobbled by an infected blister on his heel, was wearing bedroom slippers.

3. Stephen W. Sears, *Landscape Turned Red: The Battle of Antietam* (New York: Ticknor & Fields, 1983), pp. 83, 86.

4. The marches of the several columns are outlined in Freeman, *R. E. Lee*, vol. 2, pp. 363-64.

5. John Gibbon, *Personal Recollections of the Civil War* (New York: G. P. Putnam's Sons, 1928), p. 73.

6. Jackson reported the capture in his typically religious way: "Through God's blessing, Harper's Ferry and its garrison are to be surrendered" (*Official Records*, vol. 19, pt. 1, p. 951).

7. Stephen W. Sears, *George B. McClellan: The Young Napoleon* (New York: Ticknor & Fields, 1988), p. 21.

8. Freeman, *R. E. Lee*, vol. 2, p. 378.

9. Lee, *Recollections*, p. 78.

10. Marrin, *Virginia's General*, p. 71.

11. *Southern Historical Society Papers*, vol. 10 (1882), p. 503.

12. Long, *Memoirs*, p. 222.

13. Henry Adams, *Letters of Henry Adams* (Boston: Houghton Mifflin, 1930-38), vol. 1, p. 327.

14. Freeman, *Lee of Virginia*, p. 98.

15. Taylor, *Duty Faithfully Performed*, p. 104.

16. William Stanley Hoole, *Lawley Covers the Confederacy* (Tuscaloosa, AL: Confederate Publishing Co., 1964), p. 31.

17. Fitzhugh Lee, *General Lee* (New York: D. Appleton, 1894), pp. 234–35.

18. Lincoln, *Collected Works*, vol. 5, p. 474.

19. Johnson and Buel, *Battles and Leaders*, vol. 2, p. 70.

20. Cooke, *Lee*, p. 177.

21. Johnson and Buel, *Battles and Leaders*, vol. 3, p. 81.

22. Freeman, *R. E. Lee*, vol. 2, p. 470.

23. Cooke, *Lee*, p. 184.

24. Francis Augustin O'Reilly, *The Fredericksburg Campaign* (Baton Rouge: Louisiana State University Press, 2003), pp. 438–39.

25. Freeman, *Lee of Virginia*, p. 104.

26. Lee, *Wartime Papers*, p. 389.

Chapter 6: Loss of an Arm

1. Robert Beechum, *As If It Were Glory: Robert Beechum's Civil War from the Iron Brigade to the Black Regiments* (Madison, WI: Madison House, 1998), p. 38.

2. Freeman, *Lee of Virginia*, p. 105.

3. Lee, *Wartime Papers*, p. 401.

4. Freeman, *Lee of Virginia*, p. 108.

5. Spencer G. Welch, *A Confederate Surgeon's Letters to His Wife* (New York: Neale, 1911), p. 39.

6. David E. Johnston, *The Story of a Confederate Boy in the Civil War* (Portland, OR: Glass & Prudhomme, 1914), p. 174.

7. James I. Robertson Jr., *Soldiers Blue and Gray* (Columbia: University of South Carolina Press, 1988), pp. 85–86.

8. Freeman, *R. E. Lee*, vol. 2, p. 496.

9. Ibid., vol. 2, p. 503.

10. Samuel M. Bemiss to his children, April 10, 1863, Bemiss Family Papers, Virginia Historical Society.

11. Lafayette McLaws, *A Soldier's General* (Chapel Hill: University of North Carolina Press, 2002), p. 176.

12. Alexander, *Fighting for the Confederacy*, p. 195.

13. Stephen W. Sears, *Chancellorsville* (New York: Houghton Mifflin, 1996), p. 120.

14. Roland, *Reflections*, p. 52.

15. Freeman, *R. E. Lee*, vol. 2, pp. 523–24.

16. James I. Robertson Jr., *Stonewall Jackson: The Man, the Soldier, the Legend* (New York: Macmillan USA, 1997), p. 718.

17. Johnson and Buel, *Battles and Leaders*, vol. 3, p. 206.

18. Ibid., vol. 3, p. 183.

19. For details of Jackson's wounding, see James I. Robertson Jr., *Standing Like a Stone Wall: The Life of General Thomas J. Jackson* (New York: Atheneum, 2001), pp. 158–60.

20. Freeman, *R. E. Lee*, vol. 2, p. 542.

21. R. W. York to G. W. Custis Lee, November 28, 1872, letter in possession of Vicki Heilig, Germantown, Maryland.

22. Robert L. Dabney, *Life and Campaigns of Lieut.-Gen. Thomas J. Jackson* (New York: Blalock & Co., 1866), p. 716.

23. Roland, *Reflections*, p. 54.

24. Robertson, *Stonewall Jackson*, pp. 509, 754.

Chapter 7: Gettysburg

1. James I. Robertson Jr., *General A. P. Hill: The Story of a Confederate Warrior* (New York: Random House, 1987), p. 133.

2. Daniel Lyon to Annie Lyon, May 14, 1863, Eppes Family Papers, Virginia Historical Society.

3. See Lee, *Wartime Papers*, p. 490; *Southern Historical Society Papers*, vol. 4 (1877), p. 160.

4. Freeman, *R. E. Lee*, vol. 3, p. 64.

5. Gary W. Gallagher, ed., *The First Day at Gettysburg* (Kent, OH: Kent State University Press, 1992), p. 67.

6. *Southern Historical Society Papers*, vol. 5, (1878), p. 92.

7. G. Moxley Sorrel, *Recollections of a Confederate Staff Officer* (Jackson, TN: McCowat-Mercer Press, 1958), p. 157.

8. Freeman, *R. E. Lee*, vol. 3, p. 139. In his official report of the Pennsylvania campaign Lee was more severe. "The movements of the army preceding the battle of Gettysburg had been much embarrassed by the absence of the cavalry" (Lee, *Wartime Papers*, p. 580).

9. *Southern Historical Society Papers*, vol. 31, (1909), p. 234.

10. For the criticisms of Lee, see Thomas, *Robert E. Lee*, p. 303.

11. Roland, *Reflections*, p. 65.

12. Justus Scheibert, *Seven Months in the Rebel States During the North American War, 1863* (Tuscaloosa, AL: Confederate Publishing Co., 1958), p. 119.

13. Long, *Memoirs*, p. 302.

Chapter 8: Forced on the Defensive

1. Lee, *Wartime Papers*, pp. 589–90.

2. *Official Records*, vol. 29, pt. 2, p. 640.

3. C. Irvine Walker, *Life of General R. H. Anderson* (Charleston, SC: Art Publishing Co., 1917), p. 149.

4. Freeman, *R. E. Lee*, vol. 3, p. 171.

5. *Official Records*, vol. 33, p. 1275.

6. Robertson, *Soldiers Blue and Gray*, pp. 187–89.

7. Freeman, *R. E. Lee*, vol. 3, pp. 211–14.

8. Henry V. McCrea, *Red Dirt and Isinglass: A Wartime Biography of a Confederate Soldier* (privately printed, 1992), p. 431.

9. J.William Jones, *Personal Reminiscences, Anecdotes, and Letters of General Robert E. Lee* (New York: D. Appleton, 1875), p. 319.

10. Thomas, *Robert E. Lee*, p. 319; Lee, *Wartime Papers*, pp. 681, 705, 810, 814, 818.

11. Freeman, *R. E. Lee*, vol. 3, p. 268.

12. *Official Records*, vol. 33, p. 828.

13. Marrin, *Virginia's General*, p. 156.

14. *Southern Historical Society Papers*, vol. 14 (1886), pp. 525–26. This was the first of four "Lee to the rear" incidents in the 1864 fighting.

15. Taylor, *Duty Faithfully Performed*, p. 174.

16. *Southern Historical Society Papers*, vol. 32 (1904), pp. 203.

17. *Confederate Reminiscences and Letters, 1861–1865* (Atlanta: Georgia Division, United Daughters of the Confederacy, 1995–2003), vol. 1 (1995), p. 18.

18. Henry Heth, *The Memoirs of Henry Heth* (Westport, CT: Greenwood Press, 1974), pp. 186–87.

19. Freeman, *R. E. Lee*, vol. 3, pp. 352–53.

20. Ibid., vol. 3, p. 356.

21. Marrin, *Virginia's General*, p. 164

22. Johnson and Buel, *Battles and Leaders*, vol. 4, p. 231.

23. Lee was painfully aware of all of this; see Lee, *Wartime Papers*, pp. 759–60.

24. Noah Andre Trudeau, *The Last Citadel* (Boston: Little, Brown, 1991), p. 240.

Chapter 9: From Siege to Defeat

1. Taylor, *Duty Faithfully Performed*, p. 191.

2. Freeman, *Lee of Virginia*, pp. 167–68.

3. Robert E. Lee, *Lee's Dispatches: Unpublished Letters of General Robert E. Lee* (New York: G. P. Putnam's Sons, 1915), p. 254.

4. Freeman, *R. E. Lee*, vol. 3, p. 538.

5. Cooke, *Lee*, pp. 428, 430.

6. *Official Records*, Ser. IV, vol. 3, pp. 1012–13.

7. Freeman, *R. E. Lee*, vol. 4, p. 31.

8. Taylor, *General Lee*, p. 275.

9. Charles Bracelen Flood, *Lee: The Last Years* (Boston: Houghton Mifflin, 1981), p. 20.

10. Alexander, *Fighting for the Confederacy*, p. 532.

11. Long, *Memoirs*, p. 421.

12. Freeman, *R. E. Lee*, vol. 4, p. 121.

13. Ulysses S. Grant, *Personal Memoirs of U. S. Grant* (New York: Charles L. Webster, 1886), vol. 2, p. 489.

14. Freeman, *R. E. Lee*, vol. 4, p. 144.

15. Ibid., vol. 4, p. 147.

16. Lee, *Wartime Papers*, pp. 934-35.

Chapter 10: National Symbol

1. Charles Francis Adams, *Lee's Centennial: An Address* (Chicago: Americana House, 1948), pp. 56–57.

2. Freeman, *R. E. Lee*, vol. 4, pp. 196, 208.

3. Freeman, *Lee of Virginia*, p. 210.

4. Thomas, *Robert E. Lee*, p. 372.

5. Lee, *Recollections*, p. 189.

6. Ibid., p. 181.

7. Kaltman, *Genius of Lee*, p. 325.

8. Jones, *Life and Letters*, p. 410.

9. Ibid., p. 411.

10. Ibid., p. 414.

11. Lee, *Recollections*, p. 193.

12. *Southern Historical Society Papers*, vol. 17. (1889), p. 245.

13. Flood, *Lee: The Last Years*, p. 254.

14. Horn, *Robert E. Lee Reader*, pp. 508–9.

15. *Current Literature* 41 (1907): 341.

16. Flood, *Lee: The Last Years*, p. 93.

Works Cited

Adams, Charles Francis. *Lee's Centennial: An Address.* Chicago: Americana House, 1948.

———. *Three Phi Beta Kappa Lectures.* Boston: Houghton Mifflin, 1907.

Adams, Henry. *Letters of Henry Adams.* 2 vols. Boston: Houghton Mifflin, 1930-38.

Alexander, E. Porter. *Fighting for the Confederacy: The Personal Recollections of Edward Porter Alexander.* Chapel Hill: University of North Carolina Press, 1989.

Beechum, Robert. *As If It Were Glory: Robert Beechum's Civil War from the Iron Brigade to the Black Regiments.* Madison, WI: Madison House, 1998.

Casler, John O. *Four Years in the Stonewall Brigade.* Dayton, OH: Morningside Bookshop, 1977.

Chesnut, Mary Boykin. *Mary Chesnut's Civil War.* New Haven, CT: Yale University Press, 1981.

Confederate Reminiscences and Letters, 1861–1865. 19 vols. Atlanta: Georgia Division, United Daughters of the Confederacy, 1995–2003.

Cooke, John Esten. *A Life of General Robert E. Lee.* New York: D. Appleton, 1871.

Dabney, Robert L. *Life and Campaigns of Lieut.-Gen. Thomas J. Jackson.* New York: Blalock & Co., 1866.

Davis, Jefferson. *The Rise and Fall of the Confederate Government.* 2 vols. New York: D. Appleton, 1881.

Dill, Alonzo T., and Mary Tyler Cheek. *A Visit to Stratford and the Story of the Lees.* Stratford, VA: Stratford Hall Foundation, 1986.

Dowdey, Clifford. *Lee.* Boston: Little, Brown, 1965.

Flood, Charles Bracelen. *Lee: The Last Years.* Boston: Houghton Mifflin, 1981.

Freeman, Douglas Southall. *Lee of Virginia.* New York: Charles Scribner's Sons, 1958.

———. *R. E. Lee: A Biography.* 4 vols. New York: Charles Scribner's Sons, 1934-35.

Gallagher, Gary W., ed. *The First Day at Gettysburg.* Kent, OH: Kent University Press, 1992.

Gibbon, John. *Personal Recollections of the Civil War.* New York: G. P. Putnam's Sons, 1928.

Grant. Ulysses S. *Personal Memoirs of U. S. Grant.* 2 vols. New York: Charles L. Webster, 1886.

Heth, Henry. *The Memoirs of Henry Heth.* Westport, CT: Greenwood Press, 1974.

Hoole, William Stanley. *Lawley Covers the Confederacy.* Tuscaloosa, AL: Confederate Publishing Co., 1964.

Horn, Stanley F., ed. *The Robert E. Lee Reader.* New York: Grossett & Dunlap, 1949.

Johnson, R. U., and C. C. Buel, eds. *Battles and Leaders of the Civil War.* 4 vols. New York: Century Company, 1887–88.

Johnston, David E. *The Story of a Confederate Boy in the Civil War.* Portland, OR: Glass & Prudhomme, 1914.

Jones, J. William. *Life and Letters of Robert Edward Lee, Soldier and Man.* New York: Neale, 1906.

———. *Personal Reminiscences, Anecdotes, and Letters of General Robert E. Lee.* New York: D. Appleton, 1875.

Journals and Papers of the Virginia State Convention of 1861. 4 vols. Richmond: Virginia State Library, 1961–66.

Kaltman, Al. *The Genius of Robert E. Lee.* Paramus, NJ: Prentice-Hall, 2000.

Lee, Fitzhugh. *General Lee.* New York: D. Appleton, 1894.

Lee, Robert E. *Lee's Dispatches: Unpublished Letters of General Robert E. Lee.* New York: G. P. Putnam's Sons, 1915.

———. *The Wartime Papers of R. E. Lee.* Boston: Little, Brown, 1961.

Lee, Robert E., Jr. *Recollections and Letters of General Robert E. Lee.* New York: Doubleday Page, 1904.

Lincoln, Abraham. *The Collected Works of Abraham Lincoln.* 10 vols. New Brunswick, NJ: Rutgers University Press, 1953-55.

Long, A. L. *Memoirs of Robert E. Lee.* New York: J. M. Stoddard, 1886.

Marrin, Albert. *Virginia's General: Robert E. Lee and the Civil War.* New York: Atheneum, 1994.

Marshall, Charles. *An Aide-de-Camp of Lee.* Boston: Little, Brown, 1922.

McClellan, George B. *The Civil War Papers of George B. McClellan.* New York: Ticknor & Fields, 1989.

McCrea, Henry V. *Red Dirt and Isinglass: A Wartime Biography of a Confederate Soldier.* Privately printed, 1992.

McLaws, Lafayette. *A Soldier's General.* Chapel Hill: University of North Carolina Press, 2002.

Millett, Allan R., and Peter Maslowski. *For the Common Defense: A Military History of the United States of America.* New York: Free Press, 1984.

Nagel, Paul C. *The Lees of Virginia.* New York: Oxford University Press, 1990.

O'Reilly, Francis Augustin. *The Fredericksburg Campaign.* Baton Rouge: Louisiana State University Press, 2003.

Pender, William Dorsey. *The General to His Lady.* Chapel Hill: University of North Carolina Press, 1962.

Phillips, David L. *War Diaries: The 1861 Kanawha Valley Campaigns.* Leesburg, VA: Gauley Mount Press, 1990.

Quintard, Charles T. *Doctor Quintard, Chaplain, C.S.A.* Sewanee, TN: The University Press, 1905.

Robertson, James I., Jr. *General A. P. Hill: The Story of a Confederate Warrior.* New York: Random House, 1987.

———. *Soldiers Blue and Gray.* Columbia: University of South Carolina Press, 1988.

———. *Standing Like a Stone Wall: The Life of General Thomas J. Jackson.* New York: Atheneum, 2001.

———. *Stonewall Jackson: The Man, the Soldier, the Legend.* New York: Macmillian USA, 1997.

Roland, Charles P. *Reflections on Lee: An Assessment.* Mechanicsburg, PA: Stackpole Books, 1993.

Scheibert, Justus. *Seven Months in the Rebel States During the North American War, 1863.* Tuscaloosa, AL: Confederate Publishing Co., 1958.

Sears, Stephen W. *Chancellorsville.* New York: Houghton Mifflin, 1996.

————. *George B. McClellan: The Young Napoleon.* New York: Ticknor & Fields, 1988.

————. *Landscape Turned Red: The Battle of Antietam.* New York: Ticknor & Fields, 1983.

Smith, Isaac Noyes. "A Virginian's Dilemma." *West Virginia History* 27 (1965-66).

Sorrel, G. Moxley. *Recollections of a Confederate Staff Officer.* Jackson, TN: McCowat-Mercer Press, 1958.

Southern Historical Society Papers. 52 vols. Richmond: Southern Historical Society, 1876–1952.

Taylor, John M. *Duty Faithfully Performed: Robert E. Lee and His Critics.* Dulles, VA: Brassey's, 1999.

Taylor, Walter H. *General Lee: His Campaigns in Virginia, 1861–1865.* Brooklyn, NY: Braunsworth & Co., 1906.

Thomas, Emory M. *Robert E. Lee: A Biography.* New York: W. W. Norton, 1995.

Trudeau, Noah Andre. *The Last Citadel.* Boston: Little, Brown, 1991.

U.S. War Department, comp. *War of the Rebellion: A Compilation of the Official Records of the Union and Confederate Armies.* 128 vols. Washington, DC: Government Printing Office, 1880–1901.

Walker, C. Irvine. *Life of General R. H. Anderson.* Charleston, SC: Art Publishing Co., 1917.

Welch, Spencer G. *A Confederate Surgeon's Letters to His Wife.* New York: Neale, 1911.

Wolseley, Garnet J. W. *The Story of a Soldier's Life.* 4 vols. Westminster, England: A. Constable, 1903.

Worsham, John H. *One of Jackson's Foot Cavalry.* New York: Neale, 1912.

Photo Credits

Boley, Henry. *Lexington in Old Virginia.* Richmond: Garrett & Massie, 1936.: p. 142

Bradford, Gamaliel. *Lee the American.* Boston: Houghton Mifflin Company, 1912.: pp. 52, 137

Cooke, John Esten. *A Life of General Robert E. Lee.* New York: D. Appleton and Co., 1871.: pp. 60, 85, 96, 105, 117

Freeman, Douglas Southall. *R. E. Lee: A Biography.* New York: Charles Scribner's Sons, 1934.: pp. 4, 29, 74, 135

George Skoch: pp. 3, 16, 83, 91

Gettysburg National Battlefield: p. 109

Johnson, R. U. and C. C. Buel, eds. *Battles and Leaders of the Civil War.* New York: The Century Company. 1887–88: pp. 11, 26, 32, 35, 42, 45, 57, 63, 64, 69, 70, 73, 76–77, 88, 92–93, 94, 101, 107, 111, 118, 120–121, 124, 127, 130, 131

Jones, J. William. *Life and Letters of Robert Edward Lee, Soldier and Man.* New York: Neale Publishing Co., 1906.: p. 133

————. *Personal Reminiscences of General Robert E. Lee.* New York: D. Appleton and Company, 1875.: pp. 10, 30–31, 136, 138

Lee, Robert E. Jr. *Recollections and Letters of General Robert E. Lee, and His Son.* New York: Doubleday, Page & Company, 1904.: p. 23

Library of Congress: pp. 20–21, 36, 48, 79, 87, 97, 98 *(center)*, 102, 128

Long, Armistead L. *Memoirs of Robert E. Lee.* New York: J. M. Stoddard & Company, 1886.: pp. 144–145

Meredith, Roy. *The Face of Robert E. Lee in Life and Legend.* New York: Charles Scribner's Sons, 1947.: pp. x, 25, 56, 141

National Archives: pp. 15, 19, 41, 46, 51, 80, 98 *(top and bottom)*, 106, 113, 114

Robert E. Lee: In Memoriam. Louisville: John P. Morton and Company, 1870.: p. 7

U.S. Military Academy Archives: pp. 8–9, 24

Washington and Lee University: pp. ii–iii, 13

Index